Foreword

Having attended the PM Society *Digital Media Awards*, I feel quite excited at how the pharmaceutical industry is starting to embrace digital channels. Noticeably, in 2012, the quality of the shortlisted entries was far superior to previous years.

I know that the often heard phrases: 'oh that looks pretty, I need one of those' and 'my company would never let us do that' are starting to become less frequent and the industry is beginning to work around some of the obstacles and marketing faux pas. After all, digital is no longer a separate entity, but an essential component of today's broader marketing plans.

So this is a book for pharmaceutical marketers (and other pharma folk I'm sure) that is called: ***Digital Unlocked – A Beginner's Guide to Digital Pharma***. Some of you may not consider yourselves 'beginners', but I am sure there is something here to learn for everyone: something to challenge your thinking and something to help.

It includes collation of topics from Faisal Ahmed and Paul Tunnah ranging from such potentially simple areas as 'start with a plan' to the more complex 'gamification' or the dark art of 'SEO'.

I hope you enjoy this book and use it as a reference for a hugely diverse range of digital topics.

Enjoy!

Carwyn Jones,
Managing Director, Channel Health and
PM Society digital interest group lead.

Content

1. Why Bother?

We can appreciate that the digital space can be a daunting place for beginners. There are so many different social media channels and techniques, plus the pace of change is ridiculously fast. Every day there seems to be a new buzzword around, the latest new social media tool has just emerged and it can feel like there's no easy place to begin and no hope of keeping up.

So, if you're not a regular tweeter, find the thought of comments appearing on your blog terrifying or simply don't know what half the new words being bandied around mean, then fear not.

We thought that by combining our respective spheres of knowledge across both pharma and the digital space beyond we might be able to offer some intelligent (we hope) thoughts as a starting point for those wanting to dive into digital pharma and social media. Therefore, we have written this short book to give some pointers to beginners. It's not meant to be exhaustive and we certainly wouldn't venture so far as to describe ourselves as 'experts' (the pace of change is so great that you're constantly learning in this area anyway), but we hope it helps you get started.

> *"There are so many different social media channels and techniques, plus the pace of change is fast"*

The first question is, of course, why should pharma bother with the whole digital and social media space? Well, if you're reading this we suspect you know it could be important, but here's our view. Today, it's easy to come out of meetings with pharma companies and service providers excited by the opportunities for creative work in the digital space, but frustrated that 99% of them won't actually come to fruition because of regulations, fears, lack of budget, etc.

But fast forward five years and imagine the following conversation:

Digital agency: *"How about a product website split into two, one half targeting HCPs and the other targeting patients?"*

Pharma company: *"Well, do we really need a website? HCPs don't even bother coming to see it. Let's communicate our drug to patients via Facebook (we can also put the SmPC up there) and let's send the clinical data direct to the HCPs' Smartphones."*

All sounds a bit far-fetched? Well, bear in mind that fast-moving consumer goods (FMCG) companies have been communicating this way for years; pharma just needs to catch up. And yes, we 'get' the whole argument about pharma being more regulated, but as information becomes more accessible, the regulations are only going to support dissemination of accurate and reliable information, not suppress it. It may take time (hence looking forward five years), but the rules will change.

However, the key point is that, as many other industries are already doing, the digital space needs to be viewed as an intregral part of marketing and communications plans rather than something separate. Ultimately, digital is another channel to complement the existing ones pharma already uses, but a very powerful one when used in the right way and increasingly the channel of choice where patients and healthcare providers expect to receive vital information.

So pharma has to change too and it has to understand digital. Forget the terms 'digital' and 'social media' for a moment and focus on the customer. In our industry, 'customers' are the HCPs (prescribers and payers) and the patients, so you have to start with them and work backwards. The digital world is another channel to help you communicate with them, in addition to existing channels such as the phone, television, print publications, etc.

"Forget the terms digital and social media for a moment and focus on the customer"

If you don't believe the power and reach of this channel, then check out the following video for some stats and to learn how the power of the customer (through social media) is changing how we do marketing from now on.

Social Media Revolution 3:

⁜ **http://youtu.be/ZQzsQkMFgHE**

With almost 500 million internet users across Europe and with healthcare being the third biggest digital activity, we hope to help you understand the potential of this space.[1] In every industry, marketing is transforming from often didactic 'chunks' of communication to long-term community generation and management.[2]

Social media is the hot topic of the moment, but as with anything new it's best to start by observing and listening. In fact, many big brands are already doing just this in a much more organised way. For example:

Gatorade Mission Control
  ＊ **http://www.youtube.com/watch?v=InrOvEE2v38**

Dell's Social Media Command Center
  ＊ **http://www.youtube.com/watch?v=w4ooKojHMkA**

At the end of the day, it's just people talking to people, which is the most powerful tool for any business if your message is right. But as the Internet Advertising Bureau's Chief Executive, Guy Phillipson, said *"change will never be this slow again"*.

"At the end of the day, it's just people talking to people"

2. Start with a Plan

It's always hard to outline a digital strategy when the rules are so ambiguous. However, it's really quite simple – the key to a good digital strategy is the end user, full stop. Just start there and work backwards.

There are so many disciplines within digital such as SEM (search engine marketing) websites, mobile websites and apps, e-detailing, social media, email marketing, website content and so on… You have to take a step back and ask *"what does my user do digitally?"* Are they one of the 4 billion mobile users in the world or one of the 2 billion that have web access via other means?

Always start with *"what's the problem?"* and *"how do I fix it?"*. Listen to the online conversations going on around your brand (see the videos in **chapter 1** on social media monitoring), then have a look at your current activities and what your competitors are doing, where you should be and when. But don't get too bogged down with the competition; stay focused on your customers.

Next, set yourself milestones on where you should be, but don't panic, digital is always in beta mode so you can always go back, amend and continue. When looking at a digital strategy, think about how you can enhance your customers' lives. As the saying goes, in 'adland' you're exposed to around 1,000 to 5,000 ads a day, so advertising has become a blur. No-one knows the exact figure, but the point is that you have to really engage with your target audience to get their attention.

For a great example of this, see the Fiat EcoDrive advert:

* **http://www.youtube.com/watch?v=SluE9Zco55c**

"When looking at a digital strategy, think about how you can enhance your customers' lives"

It's critical to think about the right channel for reaching your audience too. More than 95% of healthcare professionals regularly work online, but which sites are they visiting?

Popular sites include:

* **Doctors.net.uk**

* **doc2doc**

* **Sermo**

* **univadis (launched by Merck & Co)**

* **Medscape**

* **DXY.cn (online Chinese doctor community with 2m members)**

Statistics from 2010 tell us that 74% of physicians take information from blogs, message boards and online social networks, so have a look at what users are saying on these sites and develop a strategy that involves a social media monitoring tool for information.[3]

Recent studies have also shown that 95% of physicians use handheld devices to download applications to access medical info, so a mobile strategy has to be at the heart of your overall digital approach.[3] However, you need to think about how you can market these apps, as finding them – whether it is through the Blackberry, Android or Apple app store – can be very hard. Look at ways to get them higher up the search results – good reviews can really help.

To summarise so far, think about who and where you target, what content you use, and how you can truly engage with your audience to get them to spend more time with your brand.

Also, with more and more patients turning to the internet for information, an SEO (search engine optimisation) strategy that encompasses paid-for-search results and optimal organic listings is critical. For an example of how ingrained search is into our everyday lives, see this video:

* **http://www.youtube.com/watch?v=nnsSUqgkDwU**

Patients often turn to Google first, then see their GP armed with an idea of what illness they think they have (the 'informed patient'). When the GP gives them a prescription, they often go to Wikipedia to find out more about the drug before going to the pharmacy to collect it. So, making sure patients can access the right drug and disease information (working within regulatory bounds obviously) is critical and there are already some great examples emerging, such as the Janssen's mobile app for motivating ADHD patients.

"Recent studies have also shown that 95% of physicians use handheld devices to download applications to access medical info"

In terms of how to structure your plan, the following example is adapted from the SOSTAC planning framework and other planning models. This can be used as a template before you make the decision to go digital.

SOSTAC planning framework

SOSTAC stands for:

1. Situation analysis

2. Objectives

3. Strategy

4. Tactics

5. Actions

6. Control

1. Situation analysis (where are we now?):

* What are our digital internal capabilities and resources?

* What's the digital perception of the brand at the moment? What are customers and employees saying?

* A SWOT (Strengths, Weaknesses, Opportunities, and Threats) analysis of the marketplace

* What customer insight do we have and what do we need to get?

* What are the goals for this project?

2. Objectives (where do we want to be?):

* What do we want our customers to do and how engaged do we want them to be?

* What are the customer acquisition and retention targets?

* What are the targets for customer satisfaction?

* Do we need to be the primary resource for this subject?

* What's our value proposition?

3. Strategy (how do we plan to get there?):

* Sit in the consumer's chair and be them for a minute. A digital detail aid may not be the solution; other digital disciplines may be more appropriate

* What are the different segments (gender, interests, location, profession, age etc.)?

* Where do our customers spend their time online and what are their habits?

* Where do we target our digital messaging or product?

* What is our positioning in the digital world?

* What tools do we use?

4/5. Tactics and actions (what methods can we use to get there?):

* How do we fit this into the overall marketing mix?

* Where are we planning to implement digitally?

* Who is responsible and who reports to whom on this project?

* What are the internal resources and skills?

* What will the external agencies do?

* List the timelines.

6. Control (what's our performance?):

* What web analytics do we have in place?

* What usability testing are we doing?

* How are we profiling our visitors?

* Who is managing the analytics and how is this going to be reported back?

The biggest mind-shift for our industry is that digital is continuously in beta. It's all about launching, getting feedback and amending to make your customers' digital experience with your brand better.

You should always:

* Plan

* Build

* Test

* Launch

* Test (again)

* Get feedback

* Amend accordingly

* Test (yet again)

* Keep developing: new technologies will come along that will enhance your offering.

The digital plan structure

The following structure will help construct your actual plan:

1. The digital project's goals

2. Insight (consumer and market)

3. Your digital messaging
   (make sure you do not retro-fit printed materials digitally!)

4. Your big thinking – 'The Strategy'

5. The tactics and actions

6. Budgets.

Remember – focus on the customer and what they need rather than the latest trendy tech (the channel).

In reality there are a multitude of channels such as search engines, email, websites, microsites, social media, mobile applications, augmented reality, online video, online PR and gaming.

You have to pick the right ones to reach your customers rather than what is in fashion.

The SOSTAC Planning System was created by Paul Smith. For more information please visit his website - **www.prsmith.org/sostac.html**

3. Websites

You've convinced your boss to give you a budget for your fancy disease area website (or even brand website if you're sat in the US). Your head is awash with thoughts about what kind of features the website should have. And you are already lining up an array of award-winning digital agencies to help make it happen.

STOP!

You could be about to fall for the biggest myth on the internet – that most famous of phrases – *"if you build it they will come."* Sadly, nothing could be further from the truth in the digital world.

It takes a lot of creativity and knowledge of your proposed audience to build a website that will attract and retain users. So take some time to think about what both you and your audience want from the website.

Here are our top tips for success:

1. Content really is the king – focus on content first and design second

2. Remember that the attention span of website users is low; they don't tend to read the content but merely scan it, so make sure there are clear pointers to guide them through

3. Stick to the key points, don't just transfer your print leaflets online. Be sure to highlight keywords, use headings, write short paragraphs and use lists

4. Adverts, particularly pop-ups, can be a real turn-off, so steer clear of them unless there is a good reason

5. Whilst animated graphics and interactivity can seem appealing, try not to make the site too flashy – it needs to work on all browsers and load in a reasonable time (load time is something Google looks at). In addition, making all images clickable and with alternate text tags will ensure you are W3C compliant (**www.w3.org/**)

6. Allow scrolling and don't worry about designing the site for the CEO's 13 inch laptop screen. People do scroll top sites such as the BBC, MSN and Facebook where the content is compelling

7. Always place important content on the left or right of the page as research shows that users tend to look at the edges before the middle

8. Don't overuse colour as bright shades/too many colours can be off-putting. Simple colours with a white background can be very effective

9. Make sure the 'contact us' information is clearly visible; it makes the website appear more human and allows users to get in touch

10. If possible, feature social media tools that allow users to interact such as forums or even live chat during office hours

11. Make sure your website is built in responsive design, this allows it to automatically resize for various screen sizes and devices and always think where the user is accessing your site (think about all screens not just PC).

"It takes a lot of creativity and knowledge of your proposed audience to build a website that will attract and retain users"

Whilst rules are there to be broken and you will know of great websites that break at least one of the above, be wary of digital agencies that ignore too many of them. Are they really looking to help you engage with the users through a website that works or just win a design award?

If you do use an external agency, it's best to go in with some clear direction on what you are looking for. We know it can be tricky to know where to start and tempting to leave it to the experts. A website build can be broken down into five key stages and you should be able to get through at least the first two before asking for external help.

1. Understand your audience, write down mini-personas for them. Research their habits: when are they online? When would they have time to interact with your site? Will they mostly view on PC, Tablet or mobile? Make sure these habits are factored into your site

2. Sit down with a blank piece of paper and sketch out an overall look and feel

3. Draft out all copy for the website, play the words out as if you were a user reading them and keep it short and to the point

4. Move onto wireframes for the site appearance. There are a variety of tools available for this, with **Balsamiq** being one of the popular ones

5. Build the site based on the wireframe design, but incorporating your branding

6. Once built, check the website usability using simple tools such as Google Content Experiments or **Usabilla**.

Remember – we're all website users ourselves so a key part of the design process is utilising your own personal experience of other sites, including the ones you like and don't like. Pay attention to their layout and learn from their successes and failures.

"Remember – we're all website users ourselves so a key part of the design process is utilising your own personal experience of other sites"

Of course, there is a lot more to websites which needs to be covered separately, such as search engine optimisation (SEO) and making them mobile friendly, but we'll come onto that in **chapters 9** and **13** respectively. Here is one example of a recent pharma website:

Rheumatology-congress.co.uk (Roche and Chugai Pharma)
   ✳ **http://rheumatology-congress.co.uk**

4. Twitter

With 440 million 'tweets' sent every day and over 500,000 people joining Twitter on a daily basis, isn't this something worth considering as part of your communications?[4]

Twitter is a microblogging service that allows you to read, write or share a message in 140 characters (a *"tweet"*). Other Twitter users can subscribe to your messages by following your account, and where you follow other people, their messages will be displayed in your timeline. For a great overview of Twitter, it's worth checking out the following video.

Twitter in Plain English:
  ✳ **http://www.youtube.com/watch?v=ddO9idmax0o**

The importance of Twitter grows every day as it's an amazing service for checking out the latest information in real time (many people found out about the March 2011 Japanese earthquake on Twitter before the mainstream news channels). With tweets featuring ever more prominently in search results, it's a must to be tweeting or at least using Twitter to monitor what people are saying about your brand. Used in the right way, Twitter can be the ultimate customer service tool.

To get started, simply go to **www.twitter.com** and register to set up your account, with a username that can be personal or a brand (provided it's not already been taken). Your homepage on Twitter will take the URL format of twitter.com/ yournameorbrand. Once you have set up your account, you're ready to go and start following people or posting your own tweets.

> *"Used in the right way, Twitter can be the ultimate customer service tool"*

Like many social media services, Twitter has a whole language built up around it, so here is a glossary of some of the common terms:

  ✳ **Mention** – To mention another user in your tweet. simply put an @ sign just before their twitter username, e.g. "great article by Joe Bloggs on @pharmaphorum"

  ✳ **Retweet (RT)** – When you see a tweet by another user that you want to share, just click 'Retweet' below the message and it's displayed to your followers instantly

* **Hashtag** – Tweets can be categorised by putting a hashtag (#) in front of certain words, with users able to click on hashtags to show all tweets that include them (whether or not they are from people you follow). Example hashtags in pharma include #hcsmeu #pharma #pmbreakfast #digisick

* **Message** – You can message users who follow you with a direct message, just like email but in 140 characters. This is a feature that can be accessed on the top navigation bar once you are logged into Twitter

* **Favorites** – If you like a tweet by someone, you can save this in your favourites, by simply clicking on 'Favorite' below the tweet

* **Reply** – If you want to reply to a tweet, simply click on the 'Reply' button under the tweet and type in the box. This will automatically include @username for the person you are replying to at the start of your tweet

* **Trends** – These are the most popular topics on Twitter right now, including promoted tweets that are advertisements by brands

* **Lists** – You can create a list of people with similar characteristics so that others can follow them too, for example people in pharma you regularly follow. To create a list, simply click on 'Lists', then create a list, give it a title and description, and just start adding people

* **Who to follow** – This is displayed on the left hand side of your page and it recommends people with similar interests to follow and your tweets (including promoted accounts)

* **Links** – Adding a website URL can be done easily by just pasting into your 'Compose new tweet' box

Like any new social media site, it's very inviting to just dive in and start engaging with people. That's fine, but it's worth bearing in mind some best practices to make sure you present yourself in the right way and don't annoy people.

Our top five best practices for Twitter are:

1. **Share** – Be transparent about your brand, be honest and don't just put out a stream of sales messages. People like interaction, not marketing spam

2. **Listen** – Start off by using the search box to simply listen and observe what people are saying about your brand. Whether you like what they're saying or not, it will prove useful and let you know what people think before you start replying and commenting

3. **Ask questions** – Encourage interaction and feedback by posting questions, asking others what they think about your brand or company

4. **Demonstrate leadership** – Post articles and references that show thought leadership to your followers and original thinking

5. **Establish a voice** – Your tweets will reflect on your personality, so try not to be pushy, too bullish or offensive. It's best to simply be honest, open with your opinions and share useful information. Remember – even if you delete a tweet, others may have seen it or shared it before you delete, so think before posting!

"Be transparent about your brand, be honest and don't just put out a stream of sales messages"

It's easy to get obsessed with how many followers you have on Twitter. From a business perspective, having more followers is of course good but don't end up just chasing numbers – it's equally important what type of people are following you and how much useful interaction you have.

"Don't end up just chasing numbers - it's equally important what type of people are following you and how much useful interaction you have"

If you focus on adding value and following the tips above, people will naturally want to follow you, but you can also try the following ideas to encourage new people to follow you:

* Be authentic

* Help and answer any questions from tweeters

* Post tweets, links and references that are of interest to your target followers

* Ask people to retweet some of your messages, but do so selectively

* Join in on trending topics where you have something valuable to say (by adding your comment and using the appropriate hashtag)

* Offer prizes for the 100th follower, etc. Some will of course follow, then unfollow if you do this but you should also pick up some genuinely interested people who will stay

* Integrate your tweets into your other channels such as LinkedIn, Facebook and your website.

Finally, as well as using Twitter directly there are many third-party applications to help you tweet more efficiently, or simply keep on top of conversations through your mobile.

Some of the best tools for this include:

Tweetdeck:
  * **http://www.tweetdeck.com**

Twitter iPhone app:
  * **http://itunes.apple.com/us/app/twitter/id333903271**

More Twitter applications are being made available (although there are hints that Twitter may be moving to restrict this). A more detailed list of them can be found at **http://www.twitdom.com**

5. Facebook

Facebook is now the most searched for brand on the web, recently securing over 1 billion users worldwide and at least half of them actively accessing the site via their mobile phones, so ignore it at your peril.[5]

At a previous agency, Facebook was banned for the staff and Faisal's first mission, before even meeting new colleagues, was to get this unblocked. His reasoning was to ask how you can block something that has so radically changed the way we get information, keep in touch, interact and share information with friends, family and colleagues. At first, it was hard convincing the owners (who just did not understand the power of this amazing tool), but now they post information on their Facebook page every day and are interacting with colleagues and clients with some amazing content. Basically, Facebook is something you cannot ignore and once you embrace it in the right way, it can really help you to have a one-to-one conversation with your target market.

To give you some figures, Facebook users install 20 million applications every day and share over 20 billion pieces of content every month. Some very scary stats when compared to how little pharma has thus far embraced Facebook. So just imagine what these users are saying about your brand and products to their (on average) 200 friends. Welcome to the world of 'channel me'!

The rules, in our view, don't stop us using Facebook for disease campaigns or corporate use, so why haven't more brands and products embraced it? For example, the following page illustrates how pharma can use Facebook to good effect:

Sanofi US Diabetes:
* **http://www.facebook.com/sanofiUSDiabetes**

"Facebook users install 20 million applications every day and share over 20 billion pieces of content every month"

So how do you embrace Facebook?

The best way is to create a fan page that is within the rules of the regulators and industry organisations (specifically ensuring individual brands are not promoted in many regions) – a page that can help users in your therapy area similar to the Sanofi example shown previously.

If you want to start with the basics, we would suggest the following:

* Nominate someone who can monitor the page and respond to comments from users

* Post videos on the therapy area (people like visual content)

* Post articles from key opinion leaders and trade journals

* Post frequently asked questions on the therapy area

* Ask users what they want to learn

* If relevant, post a link to Wikipedia entries

* Use Facebook questions or polls to really interact with your users.

Most importantly, be transparent about who you are and what the page is about. Online users, whether they are healthcare providers, patients or just the general public, tend to be very savvy about company pages and can be cynical, so you need to be clear on why you are doing it.

Test what works, what type of content people are engaging in, the stats page will give you all this data.

How to create a Facebook page in seven easy steps

1. At the top of your Facebook homepage, search for 'Facebook pages' in the 'Search' box and click on the search result

2. Once on this page, click on the link at the top on the right hand side marked 'Create Page'

3. You will then be asked to select the type of page you want to create and should select the category which relates best to the audience you want to reach. Click on this category and fill in the required information

4. Once you have filled in the required information and ticked the box to agree to the terms click the button 'Get Started'

5. You will then be directed to your page. On the 'Get Started' section you will be walked through the process of adding an image, inviting your friends and telling your fans about your new page. You can skip this though and come back later if you wish

6. Your page is now complete. As an admin (page owner), you can keep coming back and updating your page as you see fit (click 'Edit Page'), including restricting who you want to view your page and managing other admin officials, or even 'unpublishing' your page if you wish to hide it for now (under 'Manage Permissions')

7. It's as simple as that. Once the page is created you can simply add images, videos and other information in exactly the same way as you do with your personal profile page.

"Once the page is created you can simply add images, videos and other information in exactly the same way as you do with your personal profile page"

Once you have a significant number of fans, you can then use the in-built analytics to monitor how your users are responding, including:

* An overview of page usage over the last week or month

* Graphical displays of user interactions (such as 'likes' and impressions)

* User demographics, allowing you to understand what your user base looks like in terms of gender, location, language and so on

* An understanding of total users versus subscribed users (e.g. casual visitors versus more dedicated followers).

Facebook will also send you weekly emails with a quick overview of the activity on your fan page.

So why wait to engage on Facebook with your target audience?

6. LinkedIn

As this is being typed, two LinkedIn emails come in from recruitment consultants and one invitation from an old collegue. Will they be ignored? NO, a response is made as soon possible.

LinkedIn has taken the business world by storm, creating a more friendly and social way to keep in touch. In many ways, it has even replaced the old business cards and Rolodex, because with over 9 million members in the UK and 161 million global users, LinkedIn is the social tool for keeping in touch in business.[6]

If you're not on board with LinkedIn, then you're in a fast dwindling minority. Like all the best online tools, it really is very simple to get started with, just visit **www.linkedin.com** to create an account, fill in your career history and education, add a picture and any other interests and that's it.

"LinkedIn in has taken the business world by storm, creating a more friendly and social way to keep in touch"

You can now add connections, simply by allowing LinkedIn to see your email address book or by using the search functionality on the site (which is a really useful feature when you are meeting someone for the first time and want to know a little about them). At the entry level, LinkedIn works by allowing you to *"see"* people within three connections of you, so you can very quickly build up a large sphere of visibility. But don't forget, search engines can index your LinkedIn profile and others can also see you, so it can help raise your personal profile – just remember to keep your details up to date.

Now that you are up and running, you can ask questions, look for service providers, update your company profile page whenever it suits, join discussion groups and search for jobs. LinkedIn also offers the ability to add many additional applications to spice up your profile, such as polls, blogs, Twitter feeds and slideshare presentations, which can all be a great way to promote yourself to your connections. To harness the power of LinkedIn fully you should look at the group functionality, a powerful feature that facilitates discussions around chosen subject areas.

You can start by joining some existing groups (many of which are now open access, meaning you don't need to be approved to join). If you want to join in the discussion, simply search for groups in your field on the 'Groups' page, or check out the 'Groups You May Like' section. You will quickly discover some popular discussions and can get involved by liking discussions, commenting or simply starting a new topic yourself.

"To harness the power of LinkedIn fully you should look at the group functionality, a powerful feature that facilitates discussions around chosen subject areas"

If you want to go a stage further and start your own group, it's quite simple:

* Hover over the 'Groups' tab at the top and click on 'Create a Group'

* Fill in the information required, such as group name, logo, description, etc.

* Under 'Access' choose whether you want an open ('Auto-Join') or members-only group (where moderators must approve those who wish to join)

* Now start letting your connections know about your new group and get the discussion moving.

However, there are some things you can do to maximise your LinkedIn group, which can perform a very similar role to a Facebook fan page if managed in the right way:

* Add keywords in the title or description of your group to increase your search rankings on LinkedIn's search section, bearing in mind who you want to discover your group

* If you have a blog or Twitter page, add the RSS feed to the group to keep the content fresh

* Send out weekly or bi-weekly messages to update members, but don't be pushy

✳ Promote your group on other channels such as your company website or blog.

Another great feature on LinkedIn is the 'Companies' page, which can be particularly helpful when job hunting or for promoting your own company. Similar to 'People', you can also follow the individual pages for a company to keep on top of what they are doing. For your own company page, you can take the opportunity to reveal some key facts about your background, top employees, post your own jobs or list your products and services (plus ask for recommendations of them).

One really useful new feature on LinkedIn is the 'Skills & Expertise' tab, found under 'More', which is a great way for individuals to keep on top of what they need for their careers; here you can follow subjects, companies and leaders in your field. More recently, LinkedIn has allowed users to endorse your skills and you can endorse theirs too.

LinkedIn has so many features and it grows daily, but like all social media websites, being on LinkedIn helps with your search engine optimisation and presence. For brands and individuals, it allows you to voice an opinion, but most importantly you can track what people are saying about your brand.

As with most social media sites, there are alternatives such as **xing.com**, which has more than 10 million users, and smaller sites such as **ecademy.com**, which promotes itself as an exclusive business network. We believe it's good to be social and be on as many sites as possible, but you have to focus on where the fish are and with almost 200 million users worldwide, LinkedIn is the leading force right now in business social networking.

"You do have to focus on where the fish are and with almost 200 million users worldwide LinkedIn is the leading force right now in business social networking"

7. YouTube

This chapter on YouTube has to start with a video. See the history of YouTube in this short piece:

YouTube Turns Five!:
  ✻ **http://www.youtube.com/watch?v=Tlmho7SY-ic**

YouTube started life only recently, in 2005, but can you imagine watching and sharing videos online without it now? It permeates every aspect of social and business life.

The day-to-day rise of online videos cannot be ignored, as it's such a powerful way of sharing information and learning. With over 72 hours of video being uploaded every minute, YouTube is the stand-out leader in this field. Some other key statistics on YouTube are.[7]

  ✻ YouTube is the second largest search engine after Google

  ✻ More video is uploaded on to YouTube in 60 days than the three major US networks created in 60 years

  ✻ 70% of YouTube traffic comes from outside the US

  ✻ YouTube is localised in 43 countries across 60 languages

  ✻ The demographic is broad, with a high volume from 18 to 54 year-olds

  ✻ It reached over 700 billion playbacks in 2010

  ✻ YouTube mobile gets over 100 million views a day

  ✻ The YouTube player is embedded across tens of millions of websites

  ✻ 100 million people take a social action on YouTube (likes, shares, comments, etc.) every week.

"More video is uploaded on to YouTube in 60 days than the three major US networks created in 60 years"

It's quite simply another social network website you cannot ignore, which already features millions of videos on healthcare, so it's time to jump in. For example, numerous pharma clients have searched for their product on the site and found videos uploaded by patients and other users on how to take their medicine or what effects it has. The scary part is that almost all of these medical videos are showing incorrect information.

"Almost all of these medical videos uploaded by users are showing incorrect information"

Finding videos of interest is easy. To search simply type a keyword, subject, or video title into the box at the top and click on the 'Search' button to return a results page, which can then be filtered through expanding the 'Search Options' menu. You can therefore amend the results to see the most viewed videos, most recently updated and so on.

So if you've got valuable, accurate healthcare information then you have to get involved by creating your channel and sharing videos. It's really simple to get started:

* Click on 'Create Account' and fill in the details to create your 'channel.' If you have a Gmail account, you can use this to create your account (but be warned, this links your Gmail address to the account and it is very difficult to change this later, so think about which Gmail to use if you are a company)

* Once you have created an account you can subscribe to other channels, comment on videos or link up with other friends on YouTube, a bit like Twitter and Facebook

* To subscribe to someone else's video stream, click the 'Subscribe' button above the video or on their channel. Their latest videos and recent shared activity will be automatically delivered to your homepage, so you can stay up to date with everything they do

* To share a video, click on the 'Share' button beneath it to get the URL code to post onto any other social media website, or you can also click 'Embed' to get the html code to play the video through your own blog or website (although some users may disable this)

* To upload a video simply click on 'Upload' at the top of the website and YouTube will walk you through the process, noting the caveats below. When uploading, videos can be in a wide variety of formats

* As a company or product, you should customise your channel with your own branding so the user knows this is a trusted website. There's a great video which talks you through the 'branding' process for your YouTube channel - YouTube 101: Customizing Your Channel:

   * **http://www.youtube.com/watch?v=NykI2cJ9o80**

"As a company or product, you should customise your channel with your own branding so the user knows this is a trusted website"

A great example of such customisation within the world of pharma can be found with **Johnson and Johnson's channel.** If you're finding it difficult to create the custom feel you want then get in touch and we'll try to help!

You can also promote your videos by using the advertising features on YouTube, get started by visiting the **advertising overview page**. Don't forget YouTube videos are automatically integrated into Google search results so you're missing a trick if you don't have a channel featuring video content.

Bear in mind you can track all the data on your videos by clicking the button marked 'Show video statistics' below the video. This will show you how many views each video is getting and can also help you to understand your audience better in terms of demographics.

"So can you afford to not have a YouTube channel?"

It would be remiss of us to not mention the pharmaphorum YouTube channel, so check out what we are doing at **www.youtube.com/pharmaphorum**. Finally, as YouTube started life aimed at 'viral' videos (those which show massive uptake and exponential increase in viewing figures), here's one of the most popular videos on the site, with almost 500 million views:

Charlie bit my finger – again!:

    ✳ **http://www.youtube.com/watch?v=_OBlgSz8sSM**

Other video channels

We should also mention (especially as we're sadly not paid by YouTube) that there are other video channels worth checking out, such as **Vimeo**, which is great for HD (high definition) videos, or **Dailymotion.com**.

8. Emerging Channels

We've covered off the leading social networking sites that can be used both at home and at work. However, new ideas are always springing up in the digital space and before we move on we just wanted to give you a quick roundup of our favourite emerging sites that are both popular and useful.

Quora

Let's start off with **Quora**, which is growing in reputation and has been featured heavily in the news. It's basically a crowdsourcing website and a great place for asking questions within the business community. However, Quora is much more than just Yahoo! Answers on steroids, due to some nifty social sharing features and the fact that it's managed to get some pretty cool people answering questions such as Mark Zuckerberg (the founder of Facebook for those who live on Mars).

"Quora is much more than just Yahoo! Answers on steroids"

Simply log into **www.quora.com** using your Twitter or Facebook details and start inviting your friends or ask questions straightaway by using the box at the top of the screen. You can also find and answer questions by typing a subject in the box at the top of the page. Since all questions are categorised, you can quickly find your areas of interest.

In addition, you can vote up or down other people's answers or even comment on other answers. It's great for starting a discussion and getting people's opinion and there are lots of healthcare-related questions being answered. Quora is a must for the pharma industry.

Ning

Ning.com has been around for a few years now and was set up by the American entrepreneur, Marc Andreessen, the man widely credited with co-designing the web browser Mosaic. Ning is the world's largest platform for creating social networking websites and is used by marketers, enthusiasts, authors, artists and actors, to name but a few groups. It's basically like creating your own Facebook.

You can edit the site to create your own branding, invite friends and colleagues to share content, upload videos, photos and other media content. In addition, you can create groups, events and blogs.

Check out:

The Healthcare Marketing Community and Blog: ning.com/
　＊**http://www.healthcaremarketing.ning.com/**

In business terms, Smart cars has a very cool Ning social network:
　＊**http://www.smartusainsider.com/**

"Ning is the world's largest platform for creating social networking websites and is used by marketers, enthusiasts, authors, artists and actors, to name but a few"

Meetup

Another great site is **www.meetup.com**. Meetup is the world's largest network of local social and business groups and a great starting point for anyone looking to organise a new place for local people with like-minded interests to get together. But if you don't fancy starting your own group, join one of the thousands that have already been set up, many of which hold regular face-to-face meetings.

You can log in using your Facebook details (spot the trend here) then simply type in your topic of interest in the search box to find other people with the same interest, or click on 'Start a Meetup Group' to create your own new group. Once registered, when you come back to log in to Meetup, it will automatically display events near where you live as a default, so you've got no excuse for sitting behind that computer all day – get out and be social!

Instagram

Instagram is a free photo-sharing program first launched on the iPhone in October 2010 and has since seen enormous growth, recently bought by Facebook for 1 billion dollars. Instagram allows users to take pictures and amend them into 70's retro Polaroid looking pictures, which you can then share with friends on your Instagram network, or tweet and Facebook your images.

Pinterest

Pinterest is the newest big kid on the block. The whole idea behind this site is that it acts like an online pinboard (hence the name), where users can share pictures and videos. Registering is simple as you can use Facebook or Twitter and adding 'pins' is as simple as typing in the URL of the webpage, before selecting the right image and giving it a description. Other users can then share and repin your pins and you can set up multiple themed 'boards' for different types of pins. It's certainly worth checking out.

So there you go – a very brief snapshot of a few emerging sites of interest. To be honest, there are so many new sites and amazing tools coming out that can help us communicate in business that this chapter could easily be 10 times longer! However, we hope you find the above sites useful in helping to make new connections, market your brand or simply keep in touch with friends and colleagues.

Google+

With over 500 million registered users we have to include Google+ but the actual usage is very low, so we see it currently as an emerging challenger to other social networks. In fact, Google+ is an amalgamation of several services so it is actually many social networking services in one.

If nothing else, it is worth grabbing your personal and corporate real estate here and checking out two of the key differentiating features – circles and hangouts. Circles are Google's way of defining different types of followers, so you can share specifically within certain groups, whilst hangouts are a neat way of doing multi-person video conferencing through the Google+ platform.

9. Mobile Apps

Let's begin this chapter with a personal story from Faisal about the start of this day...

"When I got up this morning I found myself feeling a bit groggy, so decided to check my sleep cycle app on my iPhone to see when I slept most during the night and if I need to adjust when I go to bed. After that I had a quick flick through Twitter for the most recent news and finally Facebook to see what my friends have been doing around the world – all before breakfast.

Then, as I sat on the train, I played 'Words with friends', before knuckling down to work. At lunchtime, I listened to some of my favourite tracks through the Spotify app, whilst playing a few rounds of 'Angry Birds'. Once the afternoon's work was done, my thoughts turned to dinner-time TV, so I checked out the programme schedules using the Sky application."

We don't think he is alone in his morning routine - even his 60-year-old mum has asked for a Smartphone so she can use Skype to call relations thousands of miles away, whilst she's out of the house, shopping. The digital world has shifted massively over the past few years and the mobile phone was always going to be the leader – it just took some time.

Welcome to the world of mobile apps

Back in 2006, Faisal launched the mobile site for a leading entertainment brand and had to go to each service provider and negotiate a deal, which you can imagine took quite a bit of time. Those were the days of 'on-portal', where the gateway of content was controlled by each service provider individually – something that really stopped the development of mobile phone content for many years.

The knight in shining armour arrived on the scene in the form of the dearly departed Steve Jobs and the world of mobile changed forever in 2008. Now, with over 500,000 apps on both the Apple store and Android market, there seems to be a supply for the massive demand.[8] Over a quarter of adults and nearly half of all teens now own a Smartphone, so it's time to get on board.

Most of us expect to be just as well connected on the move now as we were sat at our desks two years ago!

"Most of us expect to be just as well connected on the move now as we were sat at our desks two years ago!"

Even in the healthcare space, which you wouldn't necessarily associate as the biggest sector for mobile apps, there are currently over 5,000 apps available. With more launching every day, this number is escalating, so apps are going to play a pivotal part in the lives of patients, prescribers and the pharma companies within the next few years.

"Apps are going to play a pivotal part in the lives of patients, prescribers and the pharma companies"

Before you go diving in to produce a shiny new app, take a moment to think about what's important about your app and start with your end user in mind. Here are my top tips for designing and building that killer app:

* Make sure you design your app specifically for your market, not just in terms of their needs but also through understanding what platform they are most likely to be on (Android, Blackberry, iPhone, iPad, PlayBook, etc.)

* Use an intuitive interface. Focus on making your app work easily, quickly and elegantly. Do not try to retro fit printed or website material into an app

* Don't make it complex by adding features that are not important to the end user – it's easy to fall into the trap of thinking that more features make a better app, but the reality is that the best ones are simple and easy to use

* Develop and design in a small team, as all the worst apps are built by committee and it's a recipe for disaster

* Don't stop when you have launched your app, instead keep going by asking users for feedback, ensuring you continue to make it easier to use and establish great content

* Avoid annoying the app stores by keeping to the developer rules – make sure you read up on these before you start by Googling to find the Android, Windows, Apple and Blackberry developer websites.

What app could you build in the healthcare space and how could it deliver value to your audience? The starting point, as always with new products, is to do some research on your potential market, then check out each store to see what apps are already available to meet their needs.

Even if someone has already filled that space don't be put off – it's not about being first but about being the best to meet the end user's needs (isn't that right Facebook?) After all, if you're still focused on just websites rather than apps in 2015, you might find yourself very lonely.

Once you have built your killer app, here are our top tips for marketing it:

* Get a lot of reviews

* Promote the app for free

* Use the provider's latest features. There's an added potential benefit as Apple likes to promote apps that do so

* All app marketing is about word-of-mouth, so develop your app with this in mind

* Use social media channels

* Get a press release out there, or even several

* Ask all your colleagues to download the app and get feedback

* Advertise on the journals where your targeted audience spend time.

"If you're still focused on just websites rather than apps in 2015, you might find yourself very lonely"

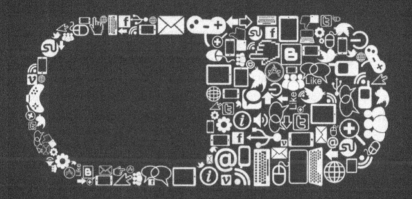

10. iPad Detailing

Apple has most definitely made an impact on pharma, as 2011 saw 50% of pharmaceutical companies moving over to the iPad, with Pfizer stating that the move would save them $500,000 per year.[9]

Those of us with a background in digital have been using apps on iPads for a few years now but end up shedding more than a few tears when pharma clients ask to take their current detail aid and just transfer it. It isn't just us – ask anyone who has worked with pharma in the digital space recently and they will tell you the same story.

It is all well and good knowing the iPad may save your company $500,000 per year, but if the detail aid was specifically designed for the iPad to use its inherent properties for interaction, you could increase sales by the same amount, adding a million dollars to your bottom line and helping educate doctors about drugs.

People ask us why we suggest using iPads – why not Blackberry or Android tablets? Well, those devices definitely have their advocates but, quite simply, no device is easier to use, faster and easier to develop apps on than the iPad. So for me, when it comes to a digital detailing enabler, the iPad wins hands down every time.

"2011 saw 50% of pharmaceutical companies moving over to the iPad, with Pfizer stating that the move would see them save $500,000 per year"

So what to do?

First of all, if you work for an agency, buy everyone in your team an iPad – designers, account handlers and copywriters. Ask them to play with it, take it home, observe how family and friends use the device and interact with its apps and watch Apple's videos on iBooks.

If you are on the client side, ask your agency or developer to show you their previous work and ask about their process for getting the campaign product live –

at this point the good ones will tell you, but the bad ones will bring out the smoke and mirrors, ducking the question.

Designing the app

Getting the design right is critical for iPad apps – they have to be user friendly. Here are our top tips for success:

* Keep it simple and check out how others are getting it right, such as Wired magazine on the iPad

* Download books and see how the best examples interact with users; get out a blank sheet and think about how you can tell a story about your product to a HCP using the device

* Don't be tempted to use the same copywriter who has written paper detail aids for years

* Think about how you will bring in key stats, references and statements from advocates

* Make sure you use the tilt and swipe features to tell your story so you get some real interactivity with the doctors

* Bear in mind that iPad design sizes are 768 x 1024 so, as a tip, design this in Photoshop and it's easier for the developers to put your product together.

Content

When using the iPad for detailing, make sure you have the mechanism of action clearly explained, as well as key advocate, KOL and HCP videos. If you are looking for examples, then a great app to reference is the Dorling Kindersley Human Body app.

Send the copywriter off to make tea or they will want to write streams and streams of copy, like they have done in the past for print. Instead, imagine yourself sat in the HCP's chair – do you really want to spend time with someone who is reeling off the same words you are reading on the screen? It's boring and a waste of time.

Development

The usual coding languages used are HTML, PHP or Javascript, all of which your developers should be familiar with. Be cautious when working with closed-loop marketing (CLM) providers, as many of them have been building e-detailing for years and their systems can be sometimes archaic. Make sure they have systems that iPad developers can really build upon and if they don't, then don't choose them as it will limit your ideas due to the lack of functionality they provide.

Some of the standard features to develop into iPad detailing include tailored presentations, call logs, CRM integration, tailored sales materials and tailored presentations that display the info the individual HCP wanted from previous meetings. The clue is in the abundant use of the word 'tailored' – don't just slap on content from other channels. Features such as pages you can email, pinch and zoom, swiping and interactive videos are all great for involving the HCP.

Training reps

Make sure your reps know how to use the iPad properly. Hold scenario sessions with HCPs to make sure you produce 'how to use' videos for the reps to view, plus have a feedback button where reps can share comments. Most importantly, don't lock the device down so you can access the iPad for only one purpose. Let the reps explore other apps so they can feed back, as a user, on how to improve your detail.

Finally, as always, launch, test and re-launch your detail aid digitally so you keep on improving, incorporating feedback and giving the reps and HCPs what they want. This will lead to effective communication and extra sales.

> *"Let the reps explore other apps so they can feed back, as a user, on how to improve your detail aid"*

Here are some good examples of pharma iPad work:

Sorted: The Daily Organiser (Janssen)
- **http://youtu.be/HOuHRn_D_CM**

myAsthma (GSK)
- **http://www.myasthma.com**

11. Gamification

Well, we couldn't really publish a book about digital pharma in 2013 without mentioning this could we? So what is gamification?

Let's start with what it's not. Gamification does not start with iPad apps, Facebook games or any kind of device – it's an approach to learning, not a technological initiative in itself.

True, gamification is a way of using technology to be more engaging, by giving the user certain actions to complete in return for rewards, but the term comes from the fact that, in essence, this replicates the interaction and reward mechanisms found in games way before the digital era.

"Gamification does not start with iPad apps, Facebook games or any kind of device – it's an approach to learning, not a technological initiative in itself"

It has become so popular because its principles contain the most fundamental human desires such as recognition, reward, competition, gifting and status.

Elements of gamification

We could write a whole book on the subject of gamification itself – actually, we would probably just build a game to teach you about it. There are literally hundreds of games mechanics principles, including complex behavioural theories and user-experience feedback. However, as a starting point the basic components of gamification can be distilled into five easy elements:

* **Progress Paths** – The use of challenges and evolving narratives to increase a task completion

* **Feedback** – Instant feedback on the users' actions, in business this is usually slow, however in gamification you need to feedback in real-time to help the user on their journey

* **Rewards** – Think of the best way to give the user a pat on the back – a target they can increase, e.g. level of power, leadership or responsibility

* **User experience** – In 2013 we have no excuse for users to not be wowed by engaging straightforward graphics and an intuitive interface that helps them on their journey

* **Social elements** – The social viral loop has to be built into your platform. A fundamental principle of games for centuries is that they have been played with friends and family. Digital and social media helps amplify this, so think about the ability to challenge people or have the ability for the user to boast about their score via Twitter, Facebook and other social platforms.

"There are literally hundreds of games mechanics principles, including complex behavioural theories and user experience feedback"

Examples

Although pharma is relatively new to gamification, there are plenty of good examples to be found outside our own industry that have already been very successful, including:

* **www.recyclebank.com** – First launched in the UK by the Royal Borough of Windsor and Maidenhead: residents get points for recycling waste that can be redeemed against vouchers to spend on the High Street

* **www.zamzee.com** – A US example, where gamification is tackling obesity by getting people off the couch to lead a healthier lifestyle. Just imagine a solution like this for diabetes sufferers or adherence programmes.

* **Idea Street** – An initiative launched by the UK Department of Work and Pensions, which challenged its workforce to come up with a new innovation management platform. Ideas for change are posted by individuals, which can receive comments and votes, resulting in leaderboards and a tie in to staff

rewards. Just imagine the possibilities for pharma if this approach was taken with sales reps around new launches, indications and training.

We are seeing the first tentative steps by pharma into gamification, with the following representing recent examples of initiatives:

* **www.syrum-game.com** by Boehringer Ingleheim. This Facebook-based game informs the public about the pharmaceutical industry. Users can track progress, exchange lab equipment, recruit lab assistants and steal scientific discoveries

* **Sorted: The Daily Organiser** by Janssen-Cilag for ADHD sufferers. A simple task-setting orientated app. Daily tasks can be categorised and prioritised and personal goals set. Points are collected as you complete your daily tasks.

"The net result – the sense of immediate reward for HCPs or patients taking part, combined with a positive impact on healthcare"

Ultimately, gamification offers our industry more than just one-off campaigns; we could use it for compliance training, research with sales reps, internal staff training and innovation. We could even evolve the HCP website and detail aid by bringing in game design principles to engage, educate and up-sell HCPs.

By adding gamification to various marketing and business initiatives we can educate, engage and enhance our customers' and their customers' experience with brands. The net result – the sense of immediate reward for HCPs or patients taking part, combined with a positive impact on healthcare.

12. Social Bookmarking

You've probably all heard the term 'social bookmarking' – some of you may be familiar with the concept but others may think it's just another current trendy web term that won't be around in 12 months' time. Well, it's not just a fad but actually a great way to organise and share content.

Social bookmarking has been around since the beginning of the commercial web, but the problem with early companies in this space was that they got hit by the dot-com bubble and were hit hard. However, fast forward a few years and they made a momentous return with popular sites such as Delicious, Furl, StumbleUpon and so on, before the real rise of social sharing took off with the emergence of sites like YouTube and Facebook.

So what is social bookmarking and what does it do?

You will have all seen the funny logos that appear at the end of news stories, blog pieces or even videos. In effect, these are a way to bookmark a particular page or piece of web content in the same way that you are used to bookmarking a page in your internet browser. But, the main (and key) difference is that you can access them anywhere where you can access the internet (irrespective of what browser you are using) and they can be public so you can share them with your friends.

> *"You can access them anywhere where you can access the internet"*

So social bookmarking is clearly useful for the user who wants to come back to their favourite bits of content. However, they are even more powerful if you are running a website – adding social bookmarking tools is great for SEO and can provide the mechanism for letting users drive your content viral. Just imagine the free exposure you're getting by allowing users to easily plug your content on their Facebook page, Twitter or LinkedIn to share it with their hundreds or even thousands of followers, colleagues or friends. There are hundreds of different social bookmarking sites out there, but some of the most popular include:

* **Delicious**: One of the most famous social bookmarking sites, claimed to have over 5 million users and 200 million sites bookmarked

* **Digg**: Another popular place where users can find and share content

* **Reddit**: Whilst it might not visually be the most appealing, this is another long-time player and very popular, so a great way to search millions of bookmarks already saved and shared by users

* **StumbleUpon**: One of the most famous social bookmarking sites that is well known for allowing its users to rate the bookmarks shared by others (socialising social).

There are always alternative bookmarking sites springing up, so some of the 'best of the rest' and newcomers include:

* **Google Bookmarks:** If you've ever starred a search result on Google or starred a location in Google Maps, it's already been saved into Google Bookmarks, so you're already a social bookmarking pro

* **Evernote**: Evernote isn't just for bookmarking web pages, you can also save components of them such as text clippings. I already know a few professional search marketers who use Evernote instead of more popular tools such as Delicious

* **Connotea**: Free online reference management and sharing for researchers and scientists, so particularly applicable in the pharma industry

* **Pinboard**: Pinboard is a bookmarking site for people who want a fast, reliable way to keep track of the things they find online without much fuss, billing itself as the bookmarking site for introverts.

For business use, social bookmarking is a must for any content you put up on the web. The great thing is that adding social bookmarking doesn't involve working with hundreds of separate sites as there are aggregator tools that allow you to add multiple icons with one piece of code.

Two of the most popular are:

* **AddThis**: A nice simple way to add multiple social bookmarks that includes all the popular ones and many you may not have even heard of. Simply click on the 'Get AddThis' button on the website and paste the code into your site. It also includes an analytics package, which is very useful

* **ShareThis**: Very similar to AddThis, but allows you to predefine which key bookmarking sites you want to include in your ShareThis box. Click on 'Get the Button' and follow the process, although it is a bit more time consuming than AddThis.

"For business use, social bookmarking is a must for any content you put up on the web"

That's a quick overview of social bookmarking, an area of the web that is only going to get more and more popular with all the buzz around social media, so make sure you're not missing out.

13. SEO

There is so much to say about the so-called 'art' of search engine optimisation, usually abbreviated to SEO, that it's hard to know where to begin. In fact, it's such a diverse and misunderstood area that companies typically just outsource it to specialists who know the area well.

In simple terms, SEO determines where your online content appears in the listings that are returned when people are trying to find something using search engines such as Google. If you get it right, you'll appear on the first page of results when someone types in terms relevant to your brand. But get it wrong and statistics say that most people won't even bother looking beyond that first page of results, so you'll probably not be seen at all. So SEO is important to ensure that you are visible on the major search engines, where Google is still by far the leader, according to recent figures by Nielson (see below).

Search engine	Market share in May 2011	Market share in May 2010
Google	82.80%	84.65%
Yahoo!	6.42%	6.69%
Baidu	4.89%	3.39%
Bing	3.91%	3.29%
Ask	0.52%	0.56%
AOL	0.36%	0.42%

Search engine market share, Dec 2010 / May 2011 (Nielson)

Even if you do seek outside expertise, it's worth understanding some of the fundamental principles of SEO, so let's start with the basics of why it's important in the first place. This video explains it far better than we ever could in words (you may remember it from **chapter 1**):

Parisian Love:

* **http://www.youtube.com/watch?v=nnsSUqgkDwU**

A lot of people now say that your brand is really what Google says it is, so don't make the mistake of leaving SEO as the last thing to do on the tick list just because you don't understand it.

> ## *"A lot of people now say that your brand is really what Google says it is"*

Just in case you're still not convinced, imagine your brand trying to make itself heard on the internet in the context of:

* 4.7 billion searches a day

* 196 million searches an hour

* 3.3 million searches per minute.

With those kind of numbers, you don't want to leave it to chance as to whether someone is going to find your page in the mass of search results.

How do search engines work?

Most search engines work by storing information about many web pages, which they retrieve from websites using automated 'bots', also known as 'web spiders', that crawl over the internet looking for key tags, known as 'meta tags', found in the titles, headings and special fields of the HTML code for pages.

This information is then stored, or cached, and used to determine when your site should be listed in a search result. Then, when a user enters a word or a string of search terms into the search engine, it examines these indexes to understand which websites provide the best match.

Of course, there is a lot more to it than just keywords. Complex algorithms are also used to determine how important or popular your website is (such as Google's 'PageRank'), which also has a bearing on how likely you are to appear high up in a search result. By the way, did you know that the term 'PageRank' has nothing to do with a page as in webpage, but is named after one of Google's founders Larry Page:

PageRank (Wikipedia):

> *** http://en.wikipedia.org/wiki/PageRank**

The search engines never explain exactly how their indexing programmes work (to avoid people trying to cheat the system with very targeted SEO) and they are constantly updating their processes, but here's a good overview video of the technology behind Google:

How Search Works:

> *** http://www.youtube.com/watch?v=BNHR6IQJGZs**

"There is a lot more to it than just keywords. Complex algorithms are also used to determine how important or popular your website is"

So where do we start?

There are over a million tips on getting your website to appear on the first page of search results, but there are some fundamental things to do that will get you started:

* Submit your website to search engines and list your site on social networks, including Google webmaster and Bing webmaster

* Have great content which is regularly updated (we recommend weekly as a minimum)

* Use title tags and descriptions. Most important is the description of your page, so make sure it's relevant to your product (this is the description that appears in most search engines under a website listing)

* Use 'alt' tags on your images – these are the keywords that appear when you hover over an image

* Get as many links coming into your site as possible, as this helps improve your SEO through increasing your PageRank (although Google is looking at this area closely, so make sure they are links from quality sites).

Have a plan!

If you are planning a new campaign or website launch, then the key things you need to do from an SEO perspective are:

* ❋ **Research** – Have a think about what search terms or words you want your website to appear under in search engine results. Try typing a few terms in yourself to see what comes back and bear in mind you're looking for no more than 15 words for your title tags

* ❋ **Get suggestions** – Google has an amazing **keyword tool** that helps you research keywords in terms of how popular and competitive they are

* ❋ **Implement** – Put your strategy into action by making sure your selected keywords are present as tags on your page. However, be patient – you won't see results straightaway and it can take months for the impact of your SEO to kick in with the search engines. Changing keywords too often means you'll never know what works!

* ❋ **Regulations** – Finally, be aware of the regulations around SEO for your region. In the UK, for example, SEO now falls under the Advertising Standards Authority (ASA), and the Office of Fair Trading (OFT) can sometimes step in.

> *"You won't see results straightaway and it can take months for the impact of your SEO to kick in with the search engines"*

Other countries will have their own regulations, but in general terms be aware of not 'misrepresenting' your product through SEO in the same way that you wouldn't in an advert.

So, we hope that's enough to get you started. You might still want to seek expert external help with SEO, but at least you'll go in with a better idea of what you need.

14. Email Marketing

To illustrate how ingrained email marketing is in our daily lives, in the last 30 minutes we have received five emails from different companies marketing their product or service to us. The cynic will say *"ah, but do you have time to read them and will you bother?"*

Actually, we might if they grab our attention – email marketing isn't dead yet and people still want to read up on subjects they are interested in. They still want to see offers and they still want to interact with your brand or product if it hits their 'sweet spot'. In fact, the old adage is that email marketing will save money on print due to the delivery efficiencies and in some industries it has become one of the most effective marketing channels. But, as with any marketing channel, if you go in with the wrong approach, it could end up costing you a lot of money for very little return.

For example, Faisal has been asked before to design a snazzy JPEG picture for attaching to an email and sending it out as part of a marketing campaign - you can probably imagine the barrage of words his account manager received.

"Email marketing isn't dead yet and people still want to read up on subjects they are interested in"

Email is no different to numerous other marketing channels in one simple respect – always think about the end user, how they interact with email and what is likely to get their attention. As a first step, it is critical to consider the fact that everyone uses different email clients such as Outlook, Apple mail, Gmail, Hotmail, Thunderbird, Yahoo! mail and some companies are still using Lotus notes.

The moral of the story is that your shiny designed-to-win-awards email may work in Gmail perfectly, but could appear broken in Outlook, so be careful to keep the design minimal and if you want to add videos or shiny objects ask the user to click-through to your site or microsite. As an aside, spam filters are getting increasingly twitchy about marketing emails and they tend to frown on attachments, links and even certain words like 'sale'.

"The moral is that your shiny designed-to-win-awards email may work in Gmail perfectly, but could appear broken in Outlook"

Here are our 13 top tips (lucky for some?) for making your marketing emails effective:

1. First of all, be relevant and always keep it in line with what your user has signed up to

2. Keep it short – if it's too long people may lose interest and say "I'll get back to that", but they rarely do!

3. If you have multiple articles or products, put a teaser on each section you write, which helps to encourage people to click through for more

4. Subject lines can be critical, so beta-test by sending two versions with different subject lines to a small portion of your database to work out which one is more effective, then use that as the final version for everyone else

5. Try keeping it to once a month, more frequent and you run the risk of being ignored as spam

6. Think about what metrics you wish to get back. The obvious ones are delivery rates, open rates and click-throughs, but you need to ensure in advance you can measure them

7. Test out the best day or time of the week to send – historically this has often proven to be Wednesday or Thursday as people are back in the swing of things with work but have time to think about other things

8. Add in links to your social media sites, or even include recent posts or tweets

9. Be very careful with the subject line as spam filters really focus on this, so avoid words like free, cheap or easy

10. Always include a link at the top saying 'if you cannot see this email, click here' and host a version on your site just in case

11. Try testing the email within your company first to see how it's received, before emailing customers

12. Design your email to be nice and simple; don't over-complicate design

13. Finally – test, improve, test, improve and repeat!

In terms of emailing systems, there are now so many cheap off-the-shelf solutions that you need to really think twice when your IT department says it can be managed internally. Remember – good external companies have experience in making sure your emails reach their desired audience and are known as 'clean' senders by the major anti-spam filters.

"Try testing the mail within your company first to see how it's received, before emailing customers"

The following companies represent just a few that offer good value solutions, but there are many more out there. All these mail solutions carry opt-in and unsubscribe tools as part of their template which helps with data protection laws.

* **www.pure360emailmarketing.co.uk**

* **www.mailchimp.com**

* **www.constantcontact.com**

15. Mobile Marketing

With all the fuss over reaching people online, why use mobile marketing? Simple – it's targeted, it's an amazing way to engage and have a one-on-one conversation with your customers, it's very cost effective if used correctly and it's a great marketing medium. Oh... and not forgetting the fact that we all have a mobile device, we carry it around with us everywhere we go, it's ultra-personal to us and we always leave it on (well, almost always).

For the last 10 years, we've had numerous conversations about mobile marketing, we've had WAP websites, we've had on-portal content and now thanks to Mr. Jobs (RIP) we have mobile apps and the rise of the Smartphone. To go into the full 'ins and outs' of how to do mobile marketing is slightly beyond the scope of this book, but let me reinforce why it's important.

There are many random stats about mobile phone usage now. Did you know there are more mobile phones in India than toilets and typically we report our phone lost or stolen to the police 24 hours before we report the same thing happening to our wallet or purse?[10]

The key thing to remember is that with mobile devices getting more sophisticated and speeds from the operators getting faster it's a medium not to be ignored. In fact, Mobile Squared reported that global mobile ad spend was £5.3 billion in 2011. By 2010, a third of agencies expected more than 30% of their clients to include mobile in their 2011 marketing efforts, so the big FMCG companies are spending even bigger money and pharma will no doubt catch up soon.[11]

> *"In fact, a third of agencies expect more than 30% of their clients to include mobile in their marketing efforts"*

If we look back at early 2011 when Smartphones really took off, Mintel reported that 45% of men owned a Smartphone, 11% an iPhone and 9% a Blackberry with O2 being the biggest Smartphone provider.[12] If we look at the UK as a reference

Western market, it is becoming hotly contested, with Google's Android operating system recently overtaking Apple as the leader.[13] Did you also know that 14% of people who access the internet on their mobile phones read fewer newspapers as a result? In fact, 16% of mobile media users overall read fewer magazines.

Finally, if you're not convinced of the power of mobile yet, then bear in mind that 89% of the UK population had or used a mobile phone in 2010 (and probably more now). The second largest activity on mobile phones in the UK is accessing news (35.5%), followed by using a browser (35.2%). Social networking was used by 22.6% of mobile subscribers in the UK in May 2010 (again, a figure which has no doubt increased since then).[14]

More specifically from a pharma perspective, figures from research conducted in late 2010 (and covered in an early pharmaphorum article named *"Smartphones: the new frontier for physicians"* **http://www.pharmaphorum.com/2010/10/12/smartphones-the-new-frontier-for-physicians/**) showed that 81% of US physicians and 44% of those in Europe had a Smartphone, with the European figure expected to have increased to at least 65% by now. From a patient perspective, it's worth noting that the NHS Direct app was downloaded over 200,000 times in the first month of launch!

The most telling statement we heard was that Google now builds all products for mobile first, so think about the mobile user before you commit to a flashy website and when you get a chance just Google the search term 'progressive design'. Google's Chairman also says if you don't have a mobile strategy you haven't got a future strategy. That's a pretty clear message and it's driven by the fact that Google now sees a billion people connecting to the web via a mobile device, up from 500 million a year before.

"Google now builds all products for mobile first, so think about the mobile user before you commit to a flashy website"

The mobile device is more than a phone, it is now your personal physician, so get your thinking caps on about what role the Smartphone can play in healthcare. Just look at some of the emerging ideas around heart rate monitoring via your mobile or those around using your pulse if you're diabetic to tell you when to take your insulin.

What's the starting point?

As always, start by asking yourself WHY?

Why do I need a mobile marketing campaign? Who am I targeting? What phone do they use and will they need my content straightaway rather than waiting to go back to a PC? With men, the predominant users of Smartphones, just think how great it would be to have sites like Pfizer's ManMOT clinic as an app or mobile site.

There are numerous types of mobile marketing to consider in your strategy such as SMS (text messages), MMS (picture messages), Bluetooth (for geographically localised things like conferences), mobile websites, mobile search and advertising, mobile video and applications and QR codes (2D pictures you see in magazines that can be scanned and take you from print to online media). The key thing when planning something like mobile marketing is to ask yourself who is in charge – IT, digital, marketing or PR? Be honest about the answer!

Most importantly, make sure you integrate mobile marketing into your overall campaign, as like most channels it's more powerful when combined with other approaches.

> *"As always, start by asking yourself WHY? Why do I need a mobile marketing campaign? Who am I targeting?"*

Do not just replicate content and stick it on an app or mobile website. Instead, play around with devices; invest in an Android Smartphone, Blackberry, iPhone and Windows phone, iPad, Playbook and Samsung Galaxy tablet so you can see how each device works with various websites.

Educate yourself – ask friends and family questions about their usage of mobile phone and start to immerse yourself in this world. It's one we're all going to be spending more and more time on.

If you keep hearing about QR codes, the acronym stands for 'Quick Response' and the code was developed by Toyota to improve efficiency in its supply chain. A user scans his/her Smartphone over the code and is directed to a website, a video, augmented reality, etc. You can create your own QR code for your brand via **http://qrcode.kaywa.com**; this can be included in all your material. You can add in KOL and MOA videos. You can add a QR code to medicine packaging and patients can store the PIL on their phone that could then tie in with adherence programs. There are many possibilities with these codes as they allow you to send big data to Smartphones instantly.

Designing your mobile site

Make sure you design your mobile site for all manufacturers:

* Use of a fluid design will help you with all the screen sizes for tablet. Make sure you design to 768 pixels wide and for 320 pixels wide for mobile

* Keep the landing page simple; make sure you have key sections in simple lists so users can get to the information fast

* Make sure the size (weight) of the page is as small as possible as mobiles have various memory sizes

* There are no special coding restrictions for your mobile site, although flash will not work on an iPhone or iPad. Use either XML or XHTML instead, with HTML5 allowing you to be more creative for the iPhone.

In terms of content, here are two quick tips:

* Keep it minimal; people are coming to your mobile site for quick information, not *'War and Peace'*

* Add your address and telephone number at the top of the first page.

SEO for mobile

Making sure search engines can find your mobile site is just as important as with a regular website, so bear the following in mind:

* Submit your site to all of the most relevant portals, directories and business listings services, as these places are also extremely important sources of mobile traffic

* Ensure that your site is 'crawlable' at the code level. Use the correct headers, don't block IP ranges unnecessarily and use the correct robots.txt file instructions

* Ensure that all of the pages you want to be indexed are situated in the public domain and not restricted by things like registration or login.

16. Online Advertising

We're all hearing big numbers about the value of online advertising – companies like Facebook and Google have made multi-billion dollar industries out of it. It's also surpassing traditional media – spending on online advertising in the UK topped £3.5 billion in 2009 and for the first time outstripped television ad spend. Back in 2000, internet ad spend was £153m, so if you get your calculator out you'll discover this means that online advertising grew by over 2,200 per cent![15]

However, what has become one of the biggest advertising channels has still to really embrace our industry. For sure, there are media sales agencies selling banner advertising, but are they really thinking about the end user or how to portray the brand message properly? Faisal sometimes refused to do online adverts for pharma due to being told to stick to a standard banner size. Try fitting all the important product information into that and it's impossible.

So what's happening is that the pharma industry is dipping its toes in the online advertising water but not really thinking about the medium – you can't put an offline advert online, full stop! The outcome – bad results and pharma dismissing the whole medium as a waste of time and money.

The key, as always, is to start with defining what you are trying to achieve with the advert and who you are focusing on. This should then drive what type of advert you run, where you run it and how you measure the results.

"The outcome – bad results and pharma dismissing the whole media as a waste of time and money"

Advert sizes and shapes

Be aware that most sites operate banner slots with standard sizes, as dictated by the online advertising regulatory bodies such as the IAB in the UK. The latest advice relating to standard online advert sizes, as taken from the IAB's February 2012 guidance, is shown overleaf.

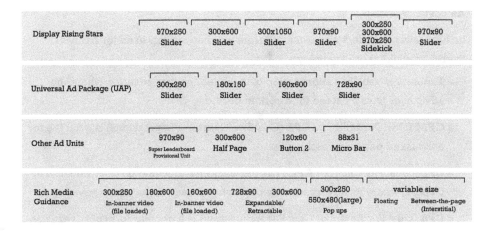

Display Rising Stars	970x250 Slider	300x600 Slider	300x1050 Slider	970x90 Slider	300x250 300x600 970x250 Sidekick	970x90 Slider
Universal Ad Package (UAP)	300x250 Slider	180x150 Slider	160x600 Slider	728x90 Slider		
Other Ad Units	970x90 Super Leaderboard Provisional Unit	300x600 Half Page	120x60 Button 2	88x31 Micro Bar		
Rich Media Guidance	300x250 In-banner video (file loaded)	180x600 In-banner video (file loaded)	160x600	728x90	300x600 Expandable/ Retractable	300x250 550x480(large) Pop ups	variable size Floating Between-the-page (Interstitial)

So if you're thinking of designing a snazzy banner advert that doesn't fit one of these sizes, then be prepared for more sites to say that they will not accommodate it.

However, bear in mind that unlike print advertising online adverts can be dynamic – e.g. they can show moving images that catch the reader's eye. Very often these can be created in flash file format, but it's always a good practice to send the advertiser a static image too in case some browsers (like iPhones and iPads) can't show these.

"A low-cost space with 10x rotation (and these do exist) will mean only one in 10 visitors see your advert"

You can also get non-banner space adverts such as pop-up (advert appears over the page), pop-under (new page opens with the advert) and interstitial (advert appears as page before the user reaches their target URL). However, bear in mind that some people find these annoying.

The cost

The next thing to understand is the different revenue models used for banner adverts (of which there are many):

* **Tenancy** is usually a sponsorship of the site or certain sections, where the advertiser pays a flat fee for a certain period

* **CPM** (Cost Per Mille) or **CPT** (Cost Per Thousand Impressions) is a flat fee for a thousand page impressions

* **CPC** (Cost Per Click) or **PPC** (Pay per click) has become popular because of Google, where an advertiser only pays when a user clicks on the advert

* **CPA** (Cost Per Action or Cost Per Acquisition) is a popular form of advertising for e-commerce sites as the advertiser only pays when a user clicks on the advert and then goes on to buy a product

* **CPE** (Cost Per Engagement) is relatively new to the ad industry – here an advertiser only pays when a user engages (usually by rolling their mouse over the advert) for around 3 seconds or more.

Overall, the most commonly used formats are tenancy, CPA, CPC and CPM (the latter two favoured by social media sites such as Facebook).

Be wary of seemingly low tenancy fees for websites with large audiences though as you may find that you are sharing one ad slot in rotation with numerous other advertisers. A low-cost space with 10x rotation (and these do exist) will mean only one in 10 visitors see your advert, so make sure you know what you are getting for your money.

The process

The normal process of online advertising usually involves someone creating the advert and delivering this to the advertiser, who normally integrates an ad serving company into their site, such as DoubleClick or ADTECH. These companies charge a fee, but also help manage the campaign and deliver reports on the results.

In addition, cookie-tracking software can be used to monitor where the results are being delivered from if the advert is being shown on multiple sites (although new privacy regulations could see this change), or different redirect landing URLs used to monitor results.

Be aware of what you say in your advert though – as of March 2011 UK online advertising has had to adhere to the strict rules of traditional media advertising, so no false or misleading product statements. See **www.asa.org.uk** for more information.

> *"As of March 2011 online advertising has to adhere to the strict rules of traditional media advertising"*

Getting results

We hope the above gives you a better view of online advertising, but the key message is to really think about the user and the website the advert is being placed on. Try running different variants of the same ad on the same site to see which yields the best results as the click-through rate (CTR) is very dependent on the ad itself.

Do bear in mind though that the CTR is typically quite low – 0.3% on average which means that three in every 1,000 people who view a banner advert click on it. But it's not all about clicks; brand association and visibility are also important and can lead to 'offline' sales. After all, it's impossible to get a direct 'click' from TV or print ads (QR codes excepted) but it still proves effective.

Ultimately, for the pharma industry to make the most of online advertising, it should work with its advertising partners to ensure that the essential product information can be communicated – this might not always fit in with a standard ad format. Maybe we should create our own ad format for our highly regulated industry rather than put a round peg in a square hole?

> *"Maybe we should create our own ad format for our highly regulated industry?"*

17. Implementation

So far we've covered a whole range of areas from websites and social media to online marketing and right through to using mobile phones for digital initiatives. By this point, you should have a good sense of what you're looking to achieve and how you plan your digital strategy.

But how do you actually implement that strategy successfully and how do you know it's working? Don't believe those who say you can't measure the return on investment (ROI) of digital and social media programmes – if you can't measure it in some way you shouldn't be doing it and there are plenty of ways to assess if what you're doing is working.

We're going to look at how you measure ROI in the digital world and why it's not just a snazzy buzz word developed by the boss so they can a) keep their job and b) keep the pressure on you! Ultimately, being able to predict ROI and then measure it in practice is critical when you're asking for large-scale investment in digital projects, particularly when the people whom you are asking for it might not understand this space, or are even totally sceptical.

So if your audience is on a forum and you have to moderate the conversation at a cost of £30,000 per year, then how do you persuade the boss to invest in that? This is particularly pertinent right now for pharma given the fact that comments can no longer be turned off on Facebook.

"Don't believe those who say you can't measure the return on investment of digital and social media programmes"

However, the fact is that a lot of emerging technologies do not show an ROI that can be measured by traditional and straightforward short term metrics. So you need to be creative in your measurement, but also take the stance of "what if I'm not there?"

If the answer is "it doesn't matter" then you're heading in the wrong direction, but assuming it does matter you need to measure that in some way.

For example, how did the agency for Barclaycard convince their client to spend thousands and thousands on a game based on their waterslide advert?

Simple – they set themselves targets based on achieving a certain number of downloads, equating to visibility for the brand.

In the end, it was the number one game in the app store for months, notching over 9 million downloads and creating far more views than the original TV advert, which probably cost several hundred thousand pounds.

In truth, ROI is very important even before implementation as it makes you think about the relevance of the project, so never dismiss it. The key though is to not get too focused on simple financial metrics, but rather focus on upstream indicators of commercial success that are more easily measurable in the short term.

Some key metrics often used in digital campaigns to measure ROI are:

* Website visitors

* Click-through numbers on banner and email campaigns

* Delivered emails

* Customer complaint numbers (low is good obviously!)

* YouTube views

* Blog comments

* Interaction on Facebook (number of comments/likes) and number of friends who actively visit your page

* Volumes of retweets on Twitter

* How many users check in on foursquare and collect points

* Time spent interacting with the digital detail aid.

So always think of the non-financial short-term element of ROI as well as the immediate financial element. Arguments around the former are not just ways to *"be part of emerging technologies"*, but should also lead to significant downstream commercial benefits. If a digital campaign engenders trust and brand loyalty, then the knock-on financial benefits could be enormous – just look at Apple.

"If a digital campaign engenders trust and brand loyalty then the knock-on financial benefits could be enormous – just look at Apple"

Most importantly, if you use websites, search engine marketing, online banner advertising and iPad detailing, the understanding of how they work together (in conjunction with offline elements) is paramount to success. One channel in isolation is rarely going to achieve the best results, so you need to measure activities as part of a coordinated marketing plan.

Practically then, if you want to check how many doctors have been influenced by your website or what they have found, via SEO, there are a number of analytical tools you can use (above and beyond Google Analytics). Many of these also integrate with existing CRM systems to allow for coordinated marketing.

Here's a few to take a look at:

* **www.google.com/analytics** – detailed measurement of website traffic, routes in, favoured pages, relevant search terms, demographics etc.

* **www.analytics.yahoo.com** – similar to Google Analytics, but developed by Yahoo!

* **www.webtrends.com** – analytics and channel management software focused more on the social side of digital

* **www.adobe.com/uk/solutions/digital-marketing.html.com** – social analytics and marketing powered by Adobe

* **www.crazyegg.com** – heat mapping for websites (showing where users focus their attention on the page)

* **www.compete.com** – competitive search and referral analytics

* **www.optimizely.com** – tool allowing comparison and measurement of different variations of websites.

However, these are all just tools – it's what you do with them that is really important. Ultimately, you should ensure you're following these steps when assessing how well the implementation is going and when measuring ROI:

* Define and challenge the metrics you are using for ROI

* Understand your audience, segment them and measure for subgroups – what works for some may not work for all

* Try out different variations on a theme, measure their impact and scenario plan on a smaller scale before settling

* Integrate all your digital measurements with offline activities

* Test and repeat!

Finally, don't forget that although the digital channels are many and varied, the approaches and logic you would apply to measuring ROI on offline initiatives should be considered and adapted, rather than dismissed. For example, defining clicks as the only important metric for online advertising may seem logical, but if you applied the same logic to print advertising no-one would ever do it!

The old adage of *"if you fail to prepare, you prepare to fail"* holds very true for digital. If you don't have clear criteria for success and a way to measure your progress against them, there is no way you can be deemed to succeed.

And you wouldn't want to stand in front of your boss with no way to show success, so make sure you plan ahead, define what success looks like and use the tools available to measure ROI. That way, even if you do fail, at least you'll know why so you can learn for next time – a concept known as #failbetter amongst the Twitter community.

"The old adage of 'if you fail to prepare, you prepare to fail' holds very true for digital"

18. Morality, Law and Codes in Digital Communication

The pharmaceutical industry works within rigid regulations that govern its behaviour in both the development and promotion of its medicines and understands all-too-well the financial and reputational penalties of getting it wrong. The digital and social media revolution therefore represents a huge challenge to the way the industry and healthcare communications agencies operate.

Whereas regulation is bounded by country borders, digital communication is boundless. Whereas regulation brings restriction to what is communicated, the internet brings freedom. For pharma there appears a magnificent opportunity to communicate alongside the spectre of swingeing regulatory retribution if that communication is judged wrong. Consequence: inaction and hand-sitting whilst the world moves on and people get their medicines information from less reputable sources.

The solution for some has been to seek more regulation: *"Tell us what we can do and then we can get creative"*. This is flawed and ultimately doomed to failure. Over the past few years the governments of Europe have been wrangling as to what information pharma companies can reasonably pass to patients (and a lot more besides). This is not an argument about whether promotion of medicines to patients should remain unlawful (all are agreed on that) but rather what constitutes promotion of a medicine by a company. Consequence: inaction and hand-sitting whilst the world moves on and people get their medicines information from less reputable sources.

What then is the resolution to this double impasse in a world where even a few of its countries cannot agree in a common cause? It is, perhaps, by re-engaging with the concept of morality.

What humans view as good or bad, kind or hurtful, wrong or right can be traced back to a few basic principles that remain very constant over time and geography, across races and cultures. Bring benefit and minimise harm to others, respect the rights of others to make their own choices and be fair in how you treat other people. Morality is about what we do to 'others'. Of course, people interpret the principles in different ways, value them differently and balance them differently so people reach different decisions about what is right or wrong, as do regulators.

There are few pharma regulations, if any, that cannot be traced to a home in one or more moral principles but we appear to have forgotten the path. Rules are meaningless without their moral foundations and are too often considered a rote-learning exercise – we can do this, we can't do that. This has tragically left us bereft of initiative when the rules aren't there.

Worse: the public, the great morass of rapidly digitally communicating beings out there don't give a fig for our rules or whether we have kept to them; they care about what they perceive to be moral. If your defence is 'We kept within the rules', when the unnameable hits the social media fan, you are lost. You may as well pack up; you have failed to act as a human.

Morality is the connection between compliance to rules and good patient and health professional communication. Compliance rules and law are born in moral principles and in particular in our obligation not to harm. Truly great communication must be ethical in that morality is concerned with our treatment of others. If you really care about your audience, if you are truly people-focused you must be acting morally.

Communicators must escape from the tragic dichotomy that currently prevails between the creative process from the compliance process. Of course, we must respect the laws and codes that apply in jurisdictions where healthcare communication is targeted but our first responsibility is to recognise those moral principles that make us human. Do that first, and not only will your activities be more likely to align with regulatory requirements wherever you are, but your communication will inevitably be clearer.

Dr. Nick Broughton
Managing Director, Pharmaceuticalethics.com

19. So Long and Thanks for all the Fish

We have covered the 'what to do' on various subjects in digital; we've given tips on what tools to use and mentioned in pretty much every section that relevance is key. Think about your end user and how they consume digital first, as you may find that the solution to your problem is not even digital to begin with. So it's over to you now to get involved. Here are some final thoughts on where to begin:

* Do your own research

* Purchase a decent report on the area (Manhattan Research have some good ones) and ask friends, family and your doctor how they consume healthcare information digitally

* We've always said being relevant is key and it's easy to test this by being a user yourself. So go out and be a gadget geek – buy a Mac, PC, notebook, tablet, get all network mobiles, get all the Smartphone operating systems and download every browser

* Test your new digital product on broadband at work, at home and before launching walk down to your local cafe and test it over their Wi-Fi network.

"The fastest growing demographic on Facebook, which has over 1 billion users, is the over-55s – how many pharma drugs are targeted at this audience?"

This might all sound like a lot of hassle, but it's a lot less hassle than seeing your digital product get just two views a month, having a bounce rate of over 30% and watching people spend less than two minutes on your site! Your product is a healthcare product and your bounce rate should be low and the time spent on your site should be high if you're a brand that helps with people's lives.

We live in a connected world now. Jersey has the second highest broadband speeds in the world, Nigeria is already testing 4G phone networks for faster mobile data and, as mentionerd earlier, there are more mobile phones in India than toilets![10]

When someone says *"we don't need that, our target audience is not using the web or mobile phones"* simply smile and run in the opposite direction. The fastest growing demographic on Facebook, which has over 1 billion users, is the over-55s – how many pharma drugs are targeted at this audience?[5]

But of course there are regulations around engaging directly with patients online. So don't shy away – get in a room full of medics, lawyers, PR, patients and regulators, and work out some solutions beneficial for everyone, without breaking the rules.

Even by 2010, there were over 150 million people in Europe surfing for healthcare information regularly and 100 million told their friends and family what they found, so think where that stat is now. We no longer just peer over the garden fence and have conversations with our neighbours, we have conversations with our 200 friends (on average) on Facebook and we tell all our Twitter followers what's going on too. With all these conversations going on around the web, do we not need a social media monitoring tool? The question more companies are asking is why did we not purchase one a year ago.

If you don't have an SEO strategy and your competitors do – where are you? How can one of the 49% of doctors who recommend branded product sites refer you to their patients?[3] Don't rely on a USB stick branded with your URL.

Find your authentic voice before joining and leading any digital conversation. Don't send emails just because it's a cheaper alternative – make sure you have the right email tool. Experiment with a small selection of the database first and then use what works best. Look to send the email out at the right time of the day, on the right day and to the right people.

Here's some food for thought – 95% of European physicians are online for professional use and the same percentage use handheld devices such as Smartphones to download applications and access medical information. The recent app by the UK's NHS was downloaded over 200,000 times in the first two weeks of launch. So do you spend 95% of your marketing budget on digital initiatives?

As a final thought, once again, be relevant to your end user – don't build it just because your competitor has. Look at what they've done and improve it. And don't do digital just for the sake of it – please think about the person suffering from the illness that your drug could help and think about if and how digital can help them.

"Please think about the person suffering from the illness that your drug could help and think about if and how digital can help them."

Never forget digital is not a one-off marketing initiative; it's a tool that carries on and on. Hopefully this book will help you deliver the best solutions that will enhance, not disrupt, the lives of HCPs and patients.

Enjoy your digital endeavours!

* Pharma marketers should familiarise themselves with their local regulations and ensure they comply with them when conducting any digital activities. Please visit www.abpi.org.uk, www.pmcpa.org.uk and www.fda.gov, or other appropriate authorities for your region.

References:

1. http://en.rian.ru/world/20120120/170857236.html

2. http://www.pewinternet.org/Reports/2010/Generations-2010/Overview.aspx

3. http://manhattanresearch.com/News-and-Events/Press-Releases/social-media-module

4. http://en.wikipedia.org/wiki/Twitter

5. http://newsroom.fb.com/Key-Facts

6. http://press.linkedin.com/about

7. http://www.youtube.com/t/press_statistics

8. http://www.readwriteweb.com/mobile/2011/10/android-market-hits-500000-suc.php

9. http://www.firstwordplus.com/the_impact_of_ipads_on_pharma.do

10. http://www.telegraph.co.uk/news/worldnews/asia/india/7593567/India-has-more-mobile-phones-than-toilets-UN-report.html

11. http://mobilesquared.co.uk/pdfs/keydevelopmentsinmobad_april2011.pdf

12. http://oxygen.mintel.com/sinatra/oxygen/list/id=545169&type=RCItem#0_1___page_RCItem=0

13. http://www.guardian.co.uk/technology/2012/feb/21/android-smartphones-os-uk-apple

14. http://www.mobilesquared.co.uk/pdfs/mobile_market_trends_uk.pdf

15. http://www.iabuk.net/about/press/archive/uk-internet-advertising-expenditure-grows-42-to-35-billion-in-2009

Glossary of Terms

3G: Third generation is the name for the enhanced data communication services that allow video calling and rich media on mobile phones. The birth of the technology led to the setting up of mobile operator 3 in the UK. We are now seeing 4G technologies emerge too.

Above the Fold: Banner advertisements that are displayed at the top of a web page. In internet marketing terms, it refers to information placed at the top of an email or web page, so that visitors see it first, without scrolling.

Acquisition Cost: The price it costs a business to gain a new customer, client, or supplier.

Ad Rotation: When a web page shows a different ad at the top of the page each time a new person views it, or when the web page is refreshed.

Ad Tracking: Method used to check how many hits or clicks an ad receives. A useful tool for discovering where the most revenue comes from, how to personalise ads to reach more people and encourage more new customers.

Adsense: Google's pay-per-click, context-relevant programme available to blog and web publishers as a way to create revenue.

Adwords: Google's pay-per-click advertiser programme.

Affiliate Program: A programme where other people known as affiliates agree to advertise for the sponsor's site. In return, they receive commission or residual payment.

Aggregation: Gathering information from multiple websites, typically via RSS (see below). Aggregation lets websites remix the information from multiple sites, for example by republishing all the news related to a particular keyword.

Aggregator: A web-based tool or desktop application that collects syndicated content.

Ad Serving: Delivery of online ads to an end user's computer by an ad management system. The system allows different online ads to be served in order to target different audience groups and can serve ads across multiple sites. Ad technology providers each have their own proprietary models for this.

AJAX (Asynchronous Java Script and XML): An acronym representing a way to create real-time web applications.

Algorithm: The set of 'rules' a search engine uses to determine the relevance of a web page (and therefore ranking) in its organic search results. (See also Organic Search Results and Search Engine Optimisation).

App: An abbreviation for application (the filename extension is .app). Applications are most popular in mobile Smartphones, however there is growing use of apps in PCs and tablet PCs such as iPads.

Avatar: A graphic image or likeness of a person that replaces a photo of the author of blog content.

Banner: Advertising method in which a web ad is placed along the top or side of a website.

Black Hat SEO: (See also SEO below). This is a popular term for SEO tactics that attempt to gain higher search engine rankings for a particular website through unethical means, such as stuffing keywords, or tricking web spiders in other ways.

Bandwidth: The transmission rate of a communication line, usually measured in kilobytes per second (kbps). This relates to the amount of data that can be carried per second by your internet connection. See also Broadband.

Behavioural Targeting: A form of online marketing that uses advertising technology to target web users based on their previous behaviour. Advertising creative and content can be tailored to be more relevant to a particular user by capturing their previous decision-making behaviour (e.g. filling out preferences or visiting certain areas of a site frequently) and looking for patterns.

Beta: First step beyond Alpha. An application (often a website) released into the public domain so it can find and fix as many bugs as possible and can be user tested. As more and more bugs are fixed, updated Beta builds called Release Candidates are created and when it is ready, the 'beta' tag is removed.

Blog: Originally short for 'web log', a blog is a web page containing discussion and opinion based articles, also known as 'blog posts' or just 'posts'.

Blogroll: A list of recommended sites that appears in the sidebar of a blog.

Brand Loyalty: The phenomenon whereby buyers prefer to purchase from a company or website based on their familiarity with it and/or its products.

Buffering: When a streaming media player saves portions of file until there is enough information for the file to begin playing.

Churn Rate: A measure of customer attrition, defined as the number of customers who cease being customers over a specified time period, divided by the average total number of customers over that same time period.

Contextual Advertising: Advertising that is targeted to the content on the web page being viewed by a user at that specific time (related to Behavioural Targeting, above).

CTR (Click-Through-Rate): A measure of the success of online advertising achieved by dividing the number of clicks on a web page, or online ad, by the number of appearances of that web page/online ad (i.e., number of impressions).

Closed Loop Marketing: Refers to the marketing process whereby data can easily be exchanged between sales and marketing, and customers can be tracked through the suspect-to-sale continuum. This provides feedback so the effectiveness of the process can be increased. Closed Loop Marketing allows marketers to measure the ROI of marketing activities and their contribution to sales and profits.

Cookie: A small text file on the user's PC that identifies the user's browser (and hence the user) so they're 'recognised' when they re-visit a site. A cookie allows usernames to be stored and websites to personalise their offering.

CRM (Customer Relationship Management): CRM refers to the complete suite of processes, methodologies, software and internet capabilities that help an enterprise manage customer relationships in an organised way. CRM often refers to a particular system such as salesforce.com, Oracle CRM or MicrosoftDynamic CRM used by sales professionals to record, track and measure the activity of sales prospects and customers.

Cross Selling: Selling an additional category of products/solutions as a result of a customer's original purchase (e.g. *"customers who bought this also bought these..."* often used at Amazon).

Crowdsourcing: A distributed problem-solving and production model. In the classic use of the term, problems are broadcast to an unknown group of solvers in the form of an open call for solutions. Users, also known as the crowd, typically form into online communities and the crowd submits solutions.

CSS (Cascading Style Sheets): A flexible system of rules that govern the appearance of content on a web page. Most modern websites separate content from style to simplify coding-making revisions. Not all browsers provide equal support for CSS – there are notable and prolific flaws in IE6.

Cost per Mille (CPM) / Cost per Thousand (CPT): Online advertising can be purchased on the basis of what it costs to show the ad to one thousand viewers (CPM). It is used in marketing as a benchmark to calculate the relative cost of an advertising campaign, or an ad message in a given medium. Rather than an absolute cost, CPM estimates the cost per 1000 views of the ad.

Conversion Rate: Measure of success of an online ad when compared to the click-through rate. What defines a 'conversion' depends on the marketing objective, e.g. it can be defined as a sale or request to receive more information.

CPA (Cost per Acquisition): Cost to acquire a new customer.

CPC (Cost per Click): The amount paid by an advertiser for a click on their sponsored search listing or display ad.

CPE (Cost per Engagement): The amount paid to engage, or interact, with a customer.

Click to Call: A service that enables a mobile subscriber to initiate a voice call to a specified phone number by clicking on a link on a mobile website. Typically used to enhance and provide a direct response mechanism in an advertisement.

Deep-Linking Advert: An advertisement that links beyond the home page to a page inside the site, with content pertinent to the advert.

Directory: A list of other websites or services online. The directory is often its own website and contains links to various sources, websites, or other information on a variety of topics.

DR (Digital Rights Management): A set of technologies used by publishers and media owners to control access to their digital content. Access can be limited to the number of times a piece of content is accessed from a single machine or user account, the number of times access permissions can be passed on, or the lifespan of a piece of content.

Expandable banner/skyscraper: Fixed online advertising placements that expand over the page in response to user action, e.g. mouse over.

Emoticons: Emoticon symbols are used to indicate mood in an electronic mode of communication, such as the popular smiley.

Favicon: An image appended to a domain name by a browser to make a website or online business stand out.

Feed: The RSS or Atom feeds used by news aggregators.

FeedBurner: A tool that enables websites, blogs and podcasts to 'burn' content into a simple form for readers to subscribe.

Feed Reader: An aggregator of content, subscribed to by the user, so that specific content or search results arrive in their reader.

FTP (File Transfer Protocol): A standard network protocol used to transfer files from one host to another over the internet.

Flash: Web design software that creates animation and interactive elements which are quick to download.

Hits: A poor measurement of activity used in Web analytics, a hit is defined as any request for a file from a Web server. If on one page you have four images, two JavaScript items and you use an auxiliary CSS file, you would record eight hits for every web visitor.

HTML (HyperText Markup Language): The coding language used to create and link together documents and files on the internet.

Hyperlink: A navigational reference to another document or page on the internet.

Impression: The exposure of a clickable ad on a website to one individual person.

Inbound Link: A link to your website from a different website.

Infographic: A graphic visual representation of information, data or knowledge.

Interstitial Ads: Ads which appear between two content pages. Also known as splash pages and transition ads. See also Rich Media.

IP address: The numerical internet address assigned to each computer on a network so that it can be distinguished from other computers. Expressed as four groups of numbers separated by dots.

Integrated Marketing: Marketing that attempts to create synergy among various online and offline channels.

Interactive Marketing: The ability to address a prospect, remember what that prospect does/ says and address the prospect throughout all interactions in a manner that lets him or her know that your organisation recalls/understands what he or she has previously revealed.

Pre-roll: The streaming of an advertising clip prior to a mobile TV/video clip. The ad is usually 10-15 seconds in length.

Java: A programming language developed by Sun Microsystems. Java is currently one of the most popular programming languages in use, particularly for server-client web applications.

JPEG (Joint Photographic Experts Group): A standard for compressed pictures, widely used on the web. JPEG is best used for photographs and other images with many shades of colour.

Keyword Density: Usually expressed as a percentage, keyword density refers to the number of keywords on a web page divided by the total number of words on the page.

Keyword Research: The research to determine the words and phrases that are most applicable or relevant.

Keywords: The words or phrases used by a prospect when performing a search. Marketers optimise their websites according to the search volumes of keywords related to their industry, product or service. Marketers can also create ads related to keywords that appear in paid search listings on the right and top of Google.

LAN (Local Area Network): A group of computers connected together, which are at one physical location.

Landing Page: A custom web page designed to convert visitors into leads or sales. Email, banner ads and even offline outbound marketing campaigns drive traffic to a landing page to capture information or trigger a sale; also called a destination page, splash page, destination URL, or target URL.

Link Building: Creating links to your website that improve its popularity (something Google looks for when rating websites).

Mashup: Combining two or more tools or services to create a whole new service.

Meta Tag: A special code or 'tag' that contains specific information about the inner workings of a website.

Micro Blogging: A form of blogging that enables users to compose brief text updates, via mobile devices, instant messaging, or email, and publish them quickly. Basically, like Twitter.

Microsite: An individual website or a selection of web pages designed to promote a specific product or service. Used to convey complicated information but limit navigation choices by not sending a web visitor to the home page of a website.

MPU (Multiple Purpose Units): A square online ad usually found embedded in a webpage in a fixed placement. Called 'multiple purpose' as it is a flexible shaped blank 'canvas' in which you can serve flat or more interactive content as desired. See also Rich Media.

Navigation: A menu of links allowing users to move from one web page to another within a site.

Netiquette: Slang for 'net etiquette', or correct/acceptable online behaviour.

News Aggregator: A web-based tool or desktop application that collects syndicated content.

Newsgroup: An email group to which people subscribe to receive news and updates.

Newsreader: A newsreader gathers the news from multiple blogs or news sites via RSS, allowing readers to access all their news from a single website or program.

OnlineAds: Online ads are generally clickable, linking to a landing page, and may include banners, skyscrapers, buttons and other formats; often animated in some way. Historic standard sizes of online ads are:
* 300 x 250 IMU - (Medium Rectangle)
* 180 x 150 IMU - (Rectangle)
* 728 x 90 IMU - (Leaderboard)
* 160 x 600 IMU - (Wide Skyscraper)
* 300 x 600 IMU - (Half Page Ad)
* 120 x 60 IMU - (Button 2)
* 88 x 31 IMU - (Micro Bar)

Open Rate: A measure of email effectiveness, the open rate indicates how many emails have been viewed.

Open Source: Describes practices in production and development that promote access to the end product's source materials. Open-source software (OSS) is computer software that is available in source code form. It is often developed in a collaborative manner and may be available within the public domain.

Opt-In: Choice that users make to willingly sign-up for emails or services online.

Opt-Out: Another term for unsubscribe from a newsletter.

Organic Search: Organic search results are listings in search engine results pages that appear because of their relevance to the search terms, as opposed to advertisements.

Outbound Link: A link that leads people to a different website from the one they are visiting.

Overlay: Online advertising content that appears over the top of the webpage.

Page View: The term used when people have clicked on or viewed a web page.

Pay-Per-Click: Online advertising where an advertiser pays a pre-agreed price each time a user clicks on their advertisement. The cost for the click is often negotiated via an auction, with ad placement determined by the relative size of the bid, as well as other factors.

Pay-Per-Impression: When an advertiser pays for their online ad based on the number of views.

Pay-Per-Lead: Paying to acquire leads from an outside party at a set rate or amount per lead.

Personalisation: Delivery of personalised content via all forms digital media.

Podcasts: An audio or video recording posted on a website that can be downloaded and played later.

Profiling: To build a picture of a target customer based on information from various sources including customer transactions, completed forms and demographic data.

Page Rank: How a particular web page performs compared with others. In the past, this was a primary measure of how well a page was rated by Google.

PHP: A programming language available in open source (to the developer community), widely used in website development.

Pop-up: An online ad that 'pops up' in a window over the top of a webpage. It is an 'interruptive' format as it intrudes on the user's browsing behaviour.

QR Code: A QR code (abbreviated from Quick Response code) is a specific matrix barcode (or two-dimensional code) that is readable by dedicated QR barcode readers and camera telephones. The code consists of black modules arranged in a square pattern on a white background. The information encoded may be text, a URL, or other data.

Rich Media: The collective name for online advertising formats that use advanced technology to harness broadband to build brands. It uses interactive and audio-visual elements to give richer content and a richer experience for the user when interacting with the ad.

Robot: Web robots, also known as internet bots or simply bots, are software applications that run automated tasks over the internet. The largest use of bots is in web spidering, in which an automated script fetches, analyses and files information from web servers at high speed.

ROS (Run of Site): An ad buying option that places an advertisement in various positions on one website.

RSS (Really Simple Syndication): An XML-based system that enables people to receive ongoing, constantly updated information collected from many sources through a simple reader.

Run of Network: This ad buying option places ads on several networked websites.

SEM (Search Engine Marketing): The process of marketing your website via search engines. It includes Search Engine Optimisation and directory submissions, as well as paid submission programs like AdWords.

SEO (Search Engine Optimisation): Adding keywords to web pages and websites (PC and mobile) so that they rank as highly as possible in search results. This is achieved through thematic page design, consistent HTML tagging, linking strategies and focusing content on core keywords.

SMS (Short Message Service): A service for sending short messages to mobile devices (mobile phones, smartphones and PDAs). The commonest form of text messaging, or texting.

Site Analytics: The reporting and analysis of website activity, in particular user behaviour on the site. All websites have a weblog which can be used for this purpose, but other third-party software is available for more sophisticated analysis.

Skyscraper: Term for an online ad format that is tall and narrow. Skyscraper ads are typically run along the right or left margin of a web page.

SMO (Social Media Optimisation): Optimising your social media page so it appears high up in search results.

Social Bookmarks: A method for internet users to store, search, organise and share web pages.

Social Media Lead Generation: The use of social media tools to support lead generation programs.

Social Media: Social media is information content created by people using highly accessible and scalable publishing technologies. Social media represents a shift in how people discover, read and share news, information and content. It has become extremely popular because it allows people to connect in the online world to form personal and business relationships.

Social Media Marketing: Engagement with online communities to generate exposure, opportunity and sales. The main advantage is generating exposure for the business, followed by increasing traffic and building new business partnerships. Common social media marketing tools include Twitter, blogs, LinkedIn, Facebook and YouTube.

Social Networking: A digital medium where people can interact with colleagues, friends and family.

Spider: Automated software that combs through websites to index web pages for search engines.

Tags: Labels or categories that describe the content of a website, bookmark, photo or blog post. You can assign multiple tags to the same online resource. Tags provide a useful way of organising, retrieving and discovering information.

Targeted: Advertising geared toward a person or group of people, identified by demographics, who would be most likely to buy a particular product or service.

Text Ad: An online advertisement that is strictly text, without graphics, sound or animation. Text ads usually appear in search results in a column next to the graphical websites (see Adsense). They download rapidly and are not affected by ad blocking software.

TLD (Top-Level Domain): The three letters at the end of an internet domain name that denote the type of organisation that owns the website. Examples are .com for a commercial organisation or business, .edu for educational institutions and .org for charities.

Unique Visitor: Website measurement that records unique IP addresses as individual visitors.

Up Selling: Selling a higher function/cost service, product or solution to a customer who is actively involved in the purchase phase of the buying process.

URL Tracking: A technology that enables marketers to determine which media are generating responses and traffic to a landing page or website.

User Generated Content: Online content created by website users rather than media owners or publishers, either through reviews, blogging, podcasting or posting comments, pictures or video clips. Sites that encourage user generated content include MySpace, YouTube, Wikipedia and Flickr.

Viral Marketing: Form of marketing that infiltrates different channels, usually for free, in the form of videos, text messages and email appends for forum posts, which are designed to be shared or passed on to as many users as possible.

Vlog: A video blog.

Wiki: A collaboratively edited web page. The best known example is Wikipedia – an encyclopedia that anyone in the world can help to write or update. Wikis are frequently used to allow people to write a document together, or to share reference material that lets colleagues or even members of the public contribute content.

Widget: A small graphical device that performs a highly focused, often single, task. Web widgets can be embedded in web pages or run on the desktop of a PC (Windows or Mac) using software such as Apple's Dashboard software or Yahoo! Widgets Engine.

Reproduced by Permission © 1994-2013 NetLingo® The Internet Dictionary at **www.netlingo.com**

Acknowledgements:

A very big thank you to Anneliese Cameron, Carwyn Jones, Rachel Farrow, Neil Copping and everyone at the PM Society; Alex Butler, Andrew Spong and Juliet Le Marque; Reg Manser for his continuous copy support; Dave Harris for his awesome designs and art direction; Fiona Fraser for her patience; Rebecca Aris and the team at pharmaphorum. And a special thank you to Nick Broughton and to Kate Pain for her dotting the I's and crossing the T's. And finally, Andrew Spurgeon for Faisal's first job in healthcare.

The **PM Society** seeks to promote marketing excellence throughout the healthcare and life science industries, promising to educate, inform and facilitate networking through its various channels – online, in print and at live events. Established over 30 years ago, the PM Society is structured around five key Interest Groups aligned to the current challenges and issues facing today's marketers – *Market Access, Digital, NHS Partnerships, Patient Engagement, Personal Development.* It is also responsible for two highly-regarded Award schemes – PM Society *Advertising Awards* and the PM Society *Digital Media Awards.* A not-for-profit organisation, the Society is run largely by volunteers with a skeleton staff working to support its growing membership. It also works closely with media partners and third party suppliers to provide quality content and workshops for members. Keep up to date with the PM Society at **www.pmsociety.org.uk**.

PriMe, the PM Society's training programme is developed by the industry for the industry addressing the specific training needs for pharmaceutical marketing and associated life sciences disciplines. Courses run throughout the year and are tailored for those new to marketing, anyone needing a refresher and advanced modules for the more experienced marketer. For more information see **www.prime.pmsociety.org.uk**.

pharmaphorum provides a digital podium for communicating thought leadership and innovation within the pharma industry. Not only does the website keep you connected with the latest trends in pharma, it can also help you develop and bring to life your own thoughts, ideas and inspirations to enable you and your business to become key pharma influencers.

In addition, the supportive digital communication services provided by pharmaphorum media complement whichever area of pharma you are in, from early research right through to late commercialisation and everything in between. pharmaphorum can facilitate in identifying effective ways to communicate your expertise to key pharma and external stakeholders online. For more information visit **www.pharmaphorum.com**.

About the Authors:

Faisal Ahmed

Faisal Ahmed is one of a handful of people in the UK who has been involved with digital for over 15 years, providing digital thought leadership to some of the biggest brands globally. He has also contributed to some of the best-selling books on digital and regularly writes for trade journals having been part of the start-up team at Amazon, defining how we shop online.

Faisal has launched digital strategies for 90 football clubs, the ECB and WRC. He also launched Playboy's mobile and social media platforms in 2006 and one of the first online social networks. Faisal has helped out James Caan from Dragon's Den on social media and has launched a series of films about diversity in advertising and regularly pushes this debate. Faisal has also been Head of Digital at Langland and Life Healthcare winning over 36 awards and has launched many firsts in healthcare such as mobile and augmented reality apps, online games and responsive designed websites. He also co-founded the first podcast on healthcare digital marketing, Digitallysick.com.

More recently he helped launch **plotr.co.uk**, a Government initiative led by industry and works with the PM Society on digital initiatives. He can be found tweeting under the username **@sickonthenet** or contacted on LinkedIn via his profile page **http://www.linkedin.com/in/ahmedfaisal.**

Paul Tunnah

Paul Tunnah is the Founder and CEO of pharmaphorum media, which provides a digital podium for communicating thought leadership and innovation within the pharma industry through both the website **www.pharmaphorum.com** and its associated media services.

Since launch in late 2009, pharmaphorum has become an established and recognised hub for discussing all aspects of pharma, with a strong focus on the use of digital and social media. In addition, pharmaphorum media provides essential support around the production and dissemination of content marketing campaigns, including expertise in social media marketing. Prior to this, Paul worked for a number of consulting organisations, including Datamonitor and IMS Health, providing sales and marketing advice to pharma companies. For queries, he can be reached on Twitter **@pharmaphorum** or through his profile page on Linkedin **http://uk.linkedin.com/in/paultunnah.**

Dave Harris

Dave is an award-winning Creative Director, Art Director and Designer and has been working above, below and online in the pharma industry for over 15 years. He can be contacted on LinkedIn **http://www.linkedin.com/pub/dave-harris/3/711/a72** and can be found tweeting **@daveaitch**.

Carwyn Jones (Foreword)

Carwyn, who has been a member of the executive committee since 2009, is Digital lead for the PM Society and works closely with Rachel Farrow on the annual *Digital Media Awards*. In 2012 he become managing director of digital channel specialists Channel Health, powered by Open Health, having spent several years at Doctors.net.uk where he was head of pharmaceutical sales and marketing.

To date, Carwyn has spent more than 15 years in the industry holding senior roles at Eli Lilly, GSK and Sudler & Hennessey. His experience covers sales, brand management, global strategy and strategic planning. A specialist in digital marketing, he also chairs the EyeforPharma European e-marketing summit and regularly speaks at international conferences on digital engagement with healthcare professionals. Carwyn is also a committed Welsh rugby fan.

Dr Nick Broughton (chapter 18)

Dr Nick Broughton qualified at Nottingham University Medical School and worked in hospital medicine and primary care for a period of seven years before joining the pharmaceutical industry.

His first role was as a clinical research manager in phase II and III studies at Sanofi Winthrop before moving into a medical adviser role at MSD UK.

He spent several years at AstraZeneca in the UK where he became Head of Medical Affairs. He then gained more than two years international experience as a Director of European Regulatory Affairs before becoming UK Medical Director at Celgene.

Nick is co-founder of **Pharmaceuticalethics.com** a company that provides education and consultancy services in ethics and compliance to pharma and allied agencies.

for babies born too soon,
too small, too sick

All proceeds from this book will go to Bliss.org.uk

Bliss is the UK charity working to provide the best possible care and support for all premature and sick babies and their families.

We believe that:

* Babies should have the same rights as anyone else

* The voices of babies and families must be heard

* Driving quality and innovation in the NHS that will deliver improved care for premature and sick babies and their families

* We achieve more by working together with individuals and organisations

* We must always be able to demonstrate the difference we make to the lives of babies and their families

Bliss is active across England, Scotland, Wales and Northern Ireland, delivering a range of nationally available services. For more information about our work in Scotland visit **http://www.bliss.org.uk/2011/02/07/bliss-scotland/**

More info on Bliss can be found here **www.bliss.org.uk**